The Art of Getting Computer Science PhD

The Art of Getting Computer Science PhD

Emdad Ahmed

ISBN: Softcover 978-1-4797-8964-1
Ebook 978-1-4797-8965-8

This book was printed in the United States of America.

To order additional copies of this book, contact:
Xlibris Corporation
1-888-795-4274
www.Xlibris.com
Orders@Xlibris.com
130233

The Art of Getting Computer Science PhD, the name clicked in my mind as per Donald E. Knuth's seminal book on *The Art of Computer Programming*. Knuth is known as god of computer science. In International Conference on Computer and Information Technology (ICCIT) (*www.iccit.org*) 2003, the first time I had written four papers, out of which only one got accepted. I was very excited to have my name as one of the authors. I remember that in the paper we used name of some other authors who had already published research papers in conference proceedings. From then on, whenever I got chance, I used to submit some research paper in the conference. To date, all the authors who were part of our published papers have completed masters/PhD at North American Universities. I feel very proud for all of them. People write auto biography when they are very famous, I understand that I am NOT famous at all, but inspired by a number of *coincidences*, I made up my mind that I will publish a book as a mixture of my personal life as well as with my computer science professional experiences that I have gone through during the last 25 years.

During Fall2010, I was appointed as an *Instructor*, Computer Systems Technology at College of Technology (COT), Montana State University Billings (*www.msubillings.edu*). The University authority was kind enough to accommodate me for the first two weeks in the *Alumni House* located at Main Campus of Montana State University Billings. I was alone in the Alumni House for the first two weeks. I came across one book left in the guest room table. The book was about life of a Montana Doctor, his untold experience for the last 40 years. I was very much inspired by all the real life stories of the doctor.

During 2011, I happened to read some of the auto-biographical books "Dream of My Father" and "Audacity of Hope" of famous American president Barak Obama. I read the book "My Life" by Bill Clinton, auto biography of George Bush etc. I also read two books, e.g., "Bankers to the

Poor" by Professor Muhammad Yunus, noble prize winner laureate, founder of Grameen Bank (www.grameenbank.com), a *pioneer in micro credit*. These are some of the books which inspired my writing. But as I told before, they are all famous people in their respective fields and they are very successful in life. I do NOT have anything other than my past 25 years of experiences of studying at four different Universities and working in various capacities as Computer Science faculty. So I decided that I will write an auto biographical book which will NOT only be my *life story* but also it might attract young people who might be interested in Computer Science *higher education* at large. My enthusiasm heavily worked when I was able to publish just a three page document titled "Teaching and Learning Computer Science for the last 23 Years" in Association of Computing Machinery International Collegiate Programming Contest (ACM-ICPC) Dhaka Site Magazine, Bangladesh during November 18-19, 2011. My fellow colleagues and students at North South University (NSU) (*www.northsouth.edu*) welcomed my writing. Actually I am very shy to write anything. I have seen some faculty write email in the group almost every day, I definitely read most of them. One of my BUET class mate and now faculty at NSU told me that I should sent the three page document in NSUALL group mail, I never did it!

I was a *mediocre* student in primary and middle school, but I used to always get *highest mark* in Science and Mathematics. I got stipend in grade eight, although my position was third in our grade eight class, only I got stipend from our school. This is a story I should share to motivate students: One day, our class teacher called all the top ranked students: *first*, *second* and *third*. From our school, it had been the cases that always the first boy gets the stipend in the competitive examination. Our class teacher was insisting that the first and second boy this time must get the stipend, mentioning no reference to me. The stipend was competitive as we had to sit for exam. I was determined to do something, studied hard to obtain stipend. Ultimately the first and second boy did not get it, only I got it. Then our class teacher said in the class that he knew I will get it! The moral of the lesson is: Just because your position is below in a class does not mean anything. Hard working and perseverance can make a difference. In my schooling, I used to participate in debating, impromptu speech, publishing wall paper etc. I was the captain/monitor of the class. I remember we organized farewell for our senior batch, stayed a whole night in school before the event. Engaging one self to social service can build leadership capabilities. Students should be involved in extra curricular activities as far as they can.

My father wanted me to be a doctor. I was admitted in Dhaka Medical College (DMC), the *top ranked* medical college in Bangladesh. Just to give the readers the idea how much competitive it was to get a chance there—out of 15000 students, only top 150 got admitted into DMC. I did NOT like memorizing huge books, so I thought medical education will not be good for me. It was a deal between me and my father, if I get admission in Computer Science and Engineering (CSE) in Bangladesh University of Engineering and Technology (BUET), only then I can quit Dhaka Medical College. As for my preparation of the above, I solved last 17 years (1970-1987) admission test questions of BUET. Fortunately, among four thousand students' admission test in BUET, I secured the *first position*. My father was neither happy nor unhappy about it. Finally, I quit DMC and get admitted in CSE, BUET (*www.buet.ac.bd*).

I did NOT even know the name of BUET until one of our neighbor in Khulna, a four year senior student to me, got admitted there. I remember when I was a student of *Lions School Khulna*, my target was to get admitted in *Govt. B. L. University College* (*www.bluniversitycollege.ac.bd*) only. I studied a lot, especially Physics, Chemistry and Mathematics during my Higher Secondary Certificate (HSC) level of education. In my Secondary School Certificate (SSC) level, although I was the *first boy* in the class, I just passed SSC with merely honors, i.e., 75% marks, whereas most of the fellow students in our class thought that I will have among some top most twenty students in *Jessore Board*. During our time (1985), there were four educational boards in Bangladesh: Dhaka, Rajshahi, Jessore and Comilla. As I did not get merit position in SSC level, I was *adamant* that I have to secure a position in HSC level and ultimately I got *fifteenth position* among 100000 students in Jessore educational Board. Soon after my passing from HSC level, I did coaching for medical admission but not for engineering admission. During our time, I think it was a record to secure *first position* in BUET admission test without doing any coaching.

University life started in August 10, 1988. I never touched computer before. I learned the programming PASCAL (**PAS**sword **CAL**culation) as the very first programming language, read a book by *Dale and Lilly*. I must confess that the way computer programming was introduced to us was not fun any more. I have seen a number of students get frustrated in computer science education just because of lack of interest in computer programming. Even I have seen undergraduate students in their final year project/thesis asking whether they can be assigned any project/thesis topic which do NOT need any coding/programming. I think Computer Science course and curriculum should address the matter, why students might not be interested in programming.

Soon after my passing from BUET in January 1994, I was appointed as *Lecturer*, Computer Science and Engineering Discipline of Khulna University (*www.ku.ac.bd*). Actually the Khulna University authority waited a bit more for our final year result to come out, as we were the *first batch* of Computer Science and Engineering (CSE) graduate in Bangladesh. In Khulna University, I conducted classes on *Numerical Analysis, Operating Systems* and *Computer Simulation*. By the way, I did my BSc. Engg thesis on *Network Simulation*. I learned how to model *stochastic process* and *event driven simulation, especially how to simulate a closed queuing network using M/M/1 Queue model*. The system uses a model of service arrival and departure rate as *Poisson distribution*. The queuing model has *closed form solution*. The similar flavor can be found now-a-days in *simulation tool* like *ns-3* and *OPNET*. My stay at Khulna University was for a very short time as I got a job offer as Local Consultant (Computer Programmer) from World Bank, i.e., International Bank for Reconstruction and Development (IBRD) assisted project under Directorate of Secondary and Higher Education (DSHE) under Ministry of Education (MoE), Govt. of Bangladesh (*www.dhse.gov.bd*). It was a good opportunity for me to pursue MS course work at BUET simultaneously with the database programming job. A B.Sc. Degree is enough for most jobs. I would recommend any students to gain some practical real life job experiences before jumping into higher studies. I gained practical experiences of Relational Database Management System (RDMBS), *facts and dimension tables, star schema* etc., as part of my job. Also I had the opportunity to handle *extract, transform and loading* (ELT) and work on *data migration* legacy system projects. Handling huge real life datasets, efficiently manage those are really worthy, it was my life time experiences. There I, in a team of international/local consultants, Data Processing Manager (DPM), computer programmers, system analyst developed Educational Management Information System (EMIS). Here I gained practical experience of RDBMS. We heavily deployed *stored procedure/function*.

I used *modulo 13 and 11 technique* for millions of automatic students account number posting. This is to say that bank and financial institutions use some *check digit* to verify that the account number is correct and append some check digit as *parity number*, the same can be re-computed if the other party knows the *formula*. I remember I had given my software free of cost to other government *projects*. As I was a very fresh computer science graduate, I did NOT have any worldly expectation other than my eagerness to continue higher education abroad. Now I understand that I did a mistake NOT to capitalize my *software patents*. I would suggest any one who can develop software, please do not forget what you have developed, make the software to use as regular service for some purposes and may be you can earn royalty/revenue out of it.

Soon after finishing masters course work from BUET, I got admitted in the Master of Business Administration (MBA) program at Institution of Business Administration (IBA), Dhaka University (*www.iba-du.ac.bd*).

Getting a chance in IBA is extremely competitive, most of our fellow engineering graduate student wish to pursue MBA at IBA. Although I was doing MBA as a part time student, I completed the degree requirements within three years, the usual time taken by a full time student. During the time I was working as Computer Programmer in Female Secondary School Assistance Project (FSSAP). It was difficult for me to convince the MBA *admission viva committee* that I really wanted to do MBA and I will finish it. I convinced them this way: Right now I am only a Computer Programmer, in our office there is a post of Data Processing Manager (DPM) who earn double the salary of mine. If I could finish MBA, may be I will be able to apply for the position. The viva committee members seem to be pleased with my answer. I think science graduate student need to learn a lot of *liberal arts*, *management* and *accounting principle* to be successful in real life. It will help them to grow as *entrepreneur* as well. I enjoyed all the 20 courses (16 core and 4 major courses) that I did in my MBA program. The strong point of a business graduate is their *smartness* and *presentation skills*. Almost all the courses in MBA required presentation of some *term paper* at the end of a semester. I learned the technique. Later, when I was working as Computer Science faculty, I always tried to assign some *group project* for the students to develop *real life application software* and make presentation in front of the whole class at the end of a semester. In a real life corporate world, a computer science graduate need to work in a team of diverse population, need to understand the client's business need and translate them into *technical/software artifacts*. These are all *software engineering* capabilities that computer science graduate must learn.

During 1995-96, I along with one of my roommate (he has completed PhD in CS from USA) heavily traveled a lot of places in Bangladesh: Cox's Bazaar (the longest sea beach in the world), Sundarban (longest mangrove in the world), Sylhet (Zaflong, Moulvibazar fall), Comilla (war cemetery, Victoria college, BARD), Mymenshing (Haluaghat). There are 64 districts in Bangladesh. I have traveled more than 40 districts. When I was a little kid, I traveled Burdwan (India) a number of times with my parents. In 1997, I visited Calcutta by Biman Bangladesh airlines (BG) and Indian Carrier (IC) as well.

Australian Government advertised for a program to do **Masters in computer science and engineering,** I avail myself of this great opportunity. I was the only person selected from Bangladesh to represent my country. In 1999, I was awarded Australian Government scholarship, Australian Agency for International Development (AusAID) scholarship to pursue MS in Computer Science and Engineering at University of New South Wales (*www.cse.unsw.edu.au*), Sydney, Australia. I stayed there for two years. In the following, I will discuss some experiences that I came across.

Although I learned C++ as the first *object oriented programming*, Java was introduced there as the first object oriented programming language. We reviewed the three fundamental features of an object-oriented programming language: *encapsulation*, *inheritance* and *polymorphism*. We had been given four assignments. I remember in a class of around 250 students, I was the one who raised hand first to report completion of any programming assignment. The first programming assignment was on *parsing* Hyper Text Markup Language (HTML) document. Actually *Web browser renders HTML document*, we simulated the same in text mode (e.g., underlining, centering, etc). *String Tokenizer* is a handy tool to automatically chop a long sentence into a number of tokens *delimited* by space, comma etc. Second programming assignment was on *Java Applet* to *simulate bouncing ball* in a rectangular region. I had used C to program *graphics driver* before, but the Java Abstract Windowing Toolkit (AWT) and later Java Swing package had a lot of built-in functionality to handle graphics rendering. *The essence of rendering a graphics object in monitor/screen is to use eXclusive OR (XOR) put*. The third programming assignment was on counting number of objects in an image and the fourth assignment was on Java Interface to test *set theoretic operations* like *union*, *intersection*, *symmetric difference* etc.

Later I also did a *summer session course* on Computer Graphics using the Java AWT/Swing toolkit. We were assigned two programming problem in Computer Graphics course: one on 2D and another on 3D objects. We developed a Graphical User Interface (GUI) editor for 2D objects manipulation etc. For the 3D part, we used technique like Binary Space Partitioning (BSP) tree algorithm for the *hidden surface remova*l etc. I remember we were given code of around 20000 lines and we had to code ourselves around 1000 lines. Still we had a hard time understanding the codes. The *instructor in charge* said that we had been given about 20 *modules*, whereas any real life application needs at least 50 modules. I also remember we had to sit for final exam as *open book*. The questions were about 12 pages and answer required only 2-3 pages! Also I remember, although the exam was open book, I did not have to open the book!

In a Database Systems course, we learned Oracle Procedural Language extension to Structured Query Language (PL/SQL). This is to say that SQL has limitation such as it can't *iterate* through record sets, PL/SQL has overcome those limitation. My understanding of *functional dependency (FD)*, normalization, relational database design theory, transaction management etc. became solid by doing the course. I remember the most difficult SQL query was a *divide operation*. Again, I was the first to report completion of all the project requirements.

I read Cormen's bible book on Algorithms as part of Design and Analysis of Algorithm course. We were given three programming problems:

word search tool (using Knuth-Morris-Pratt linear time algorithm), structural analysis tool (to determine longest shortest path of a graph (aka diameter) and to find *articulation point* of a network) and encryption and decryption of message using Rivest, Shamir and Adelson (RSA) algorithm. I knew *prime numbers* are very important, RSA algorithm uses *modular multiplicative inverse* to find the *encryption* and *decryption* key.

In Microprocessor and Embedded Systems Design course we learned *Motorola 68HC11* kit. Previously in my undergraduate studies, we learned *Intel* processor based 8086 systems. We had done a number of hands on laboratory experiments such as RS232 based serial communication, multi function timer, multi tasking etc.

In the Next Generation Database Systems course, we learned Web programming PHP, MySQL, Java Servlet etc. Also we studied object based database systems like O2, Object Store Persistent Storage Engine (PSE).

In Software Engineering course, we learned *software specification language B*. In Artificial Intelligence course, we reviewed and learned Prolog, specifically natural language understanding by Prolog program. In Neural Network course, we learned error back propagation learning algorithm for human face detection, *Elman's network*, *simple recurrent network* (SRN) etc. We also learned a package *tlearn* to predict stock share price. Just because of this reference in my CV, I was almost going to get a job offer in Australia, although due to immigration issues, I could not join the job. In Network Routing and Switching course we learned how to simulate *distance vector routing* algorithm. I should say a PhD student must go through a rigorous amount of course work, otherwise there will be lacking in theoretical understanding.

Soon after my completion of MS degree, I was awarded full funding to pursue PhD in USA. Unfortunately, I could not start PhD program in 2001. *Coincidentally*, September 11 happened and somehow become part of my life. Then I joined in the Department of Computer Science and Engineering at North South University (NSU) as *Lecturer*. In the following, I will try to recall my experiences of teaching more than 2000 students at NSU for 5 years.

Let me write something about my experiences on solving *recurrence relations*. There are three ways to solve recurrence equations: *master theorem*, *using iteration* and *substitution method*. I prefer solving recurrence using iteration and then check the correctness by applying the master theorem. I remember one problem that required to compare two alternative solutions and to recommend which solution is better/faster. The key to answer the question was to determine which one is smaller: n or $(\log n)^2$.

It was one of my favorite questions to ask in the Data Structure or Design and Analysis of Algorithms course: given a set of numbers in terms of N, $\sqrt{N}$, $N^{1.5}$, N^2, $N \log N$, $N \log \log N$, $N \log^2 N$, $2/N$, 2^N, $2^{N/2}$, 37, $N^2 \log N$,

N^3, determine the *correct order of growth*. It happened that very few students could rank all the numbers correctly.

Binary Tree traversal algorithms viz. *inorder*, *preorder* and *postorder*, was my favorite question to ask in Data Structure or Design and Analysis of Algorithms course. Although very simple to understand, the definition involved *recursion*, so most of the time students could not come up with correct sequence of nodes to be traversed. Suppose that we are given two sequences of elements corresponds to the *inorder* sequence and *preorder* sequence. Prove that it is possible to reconstruct a unique binary tree. Another popular question was for Binary Search Tree (BST), if we can maintain the *BST property*, then *inorder* traversal will yield a sorted list.

Some problems can be solved by tries all possibilities. These methods are called "*brute-force*" computing. For many interesting problems there is no known algorithmic approach other than using sheer brute force, which in some cases might be prohibitively expensive.

Recursion has elegant solution to the problems. Every recursive problem can be solved by *iterative method* as well. Let me recall all the *recursive problems* that I happened to go through and solved. By no means, the list is exhaustive.

1. factorial(n)
2. Fibonacci(n)
3. dec2bin(n)
4. largest(list)
5. smallest(list)
6. isPalindrome(str)
7. power(x, y)
8. gcd(x, y)
9. lcm(x, y)
10. multiply(x, y)
11. quotient(m, n)
12. strReverse(str)
13. TowerOfHanoi(nDisk)
14. Permutation(list)
15. NChooseR(n, r)
16. QuickSort(List, n)
17. sumList(alist)
18. Sum(n)
19. writeVertical(n)
20. SelectionSort(List, n)

There are a lot of programming languages. Followings are the most prominent. I have summarized their
Abbreviated and elaborated meaning:

a. FORTRAN **FOR**mula TRANslation
b. LISP **LIS**t **P**rocessing
c. PHP **PHP** Hypertext Preprocessor
d. BASIC **B**eginners **A**ll **P**urpose **S**ymbolic **I**nstruction **C**ode
e. PASCAL **PAS**sword **CAL**culation
f. PROLOG **PRO**gramming in **LOG**ic
g. COBOL **CO**mmon **B**usiness **O**riented **L**anguage
h. PERL **P**ractical **E**xtraction and **R**eport **L**anguage
i. JSP **J**ava **S**erver **P**age
j. ASP **A**ctive **S**erver **P**age

In computer science, we are used to two different types of solution for a problem: *greedy algorithm* and *dynamic programming*. In a greedy algorithm, which one seems promising right moment is taken in the hope of *local minimum/maximum* will ultimately reach to *global minimum/maximum*. I relate this concept in my real life, I always look for greedy solution, which seems best for me right moment, I go for it. We understand that greedy algorithm might not give us the *optimal solution*, but it can achieve near optimal solution with ease of computation. For example, *0-1 Knapsack* problem is NP hard, whereas *fractional knapsack* problem has the *greedy choice property*. By the way, in my PhD dissertation, I formulated the solution of my problem as one of the greedy algorithm which can solve the *label assignment* for the anonymous datasets problem as greedy solution. And I claimed that my solution is a *linear time algorithm*. Of course, when my assumption for *Disjoint Set Column (DSC)* does not hold, the problem will turn out to be a NP-hard problem. I took some time to explain this in my PhD dissertation *final defense* as well: my PhD dissertation committee members said, "What you did is very easy, and what you could NOT do is very difficult, how come it be!" I confidently said yes it is based on my solid understanding from the course *Theory of Computation* as well as I had a lot of reading regarding NP Completeness as part of *Design and Analysis of Algorithms* course.

I have taught a wide variety of computer science courses at various capacities. At the beginning of the semester, we used to give a *handout* to the students outlining the details of each courses. Below I am mentioning a number of such handouts, which are *legal covenants* between students and faculties.

CSC382/CSE482/ETE334
Internet and Web Technology
Fall 2011

Department of Electrical Engineering and Computer Science (EECS)

North South University

Instructor: Dr. Emdad Ahmed
Email: emdad@northsouth.edu
Tel. 8852000 ext 1535
Meeting time: MW 2:40-4:10
Office Hour: MW 11:00-12:30
Lab Hours: TBA
Meeting Place: SAC311
UGA: Saami Rahman (saamirahman@gmail.com)

Course Description

This course will provide an introduction to fundamental concepts in the design and implementation of interactive Web applications. Topics to be covered include: Internet, HTTP protocol, Web designing concept, XHTML, Server Side Includes (SSI), Cascading Style Sheet (CSS), CGI programming, XML processing, Wireless Internet, use of WML for creating WAP applications; client side scripting with JavaScript, server side scripting with PHP. Students in this class will learn not only to develop basic Web sites with XHTML and JavaScript but also they will be able to develop database backed (MySQL/Oracle/ SQL Server 2000) dynamic Web applications using PHP. Backend Database connectivity will be tested as a 3-tier model. The course will provide students with advanced programming skills to create and maintain dynamic Web sites using technologies such as Cascading Style Sheets (CSS), PHP, JavaScript and Ajax. Students will gain skills in developing interactive Web sites that perform both client-side and server-side processing while interacting with databases.

Course Description (from catalogue 2009-2010)

The course develops an in-depth knowledge of the concepts, principles and implementation techniques related to the Internet and Web technology. Details about the Internet, Intranet, Extranet, and e-commerce will be covered. Topics include Web server management, threats, security of client and server, network security like firewall, SSL, etc., authentication and authorization, legislation, privacy and IP act, electronic payment, e-business, search engine, Internet protocols like TCP/IP, SGML, XML. Design and development of Web applications using Java Applets, ASP, JavaScript, CGI and other Web tools is discussed. Prerequisite: CSE338 3 credit.

Course Objective

Upon completion of the course, students will be able to:

- Develop an in-depth understanding of Web programming technologies and tools such as CSS, PHP, Apache and MySQL.
- Ability to code HTML/XHTML/DHTML pages
- Understand the basics concepts in Web Page designing
- Design graphics and images for the Web
- Create a dynamic and interactive Web from database driven Web Page
- Understanding of advanced Web design principles including:
    - Interactive Content
    - Server side scripting
    - Styles and Themes (seperating content from style)
    - Database connectivity and management
- Ability to use Cascading Style Sheets to format a Web page
- Ability to use Javascript, jQuery, AJAX
- Ability to create dynamic Websites that utilize a database
- Experience setting up and administering Web servers
- Use various Web technologies for effective Web Page designing
- Create a Web portal.

Prerequisites

CSC311/ETE335 Database Systems and CSE338/ETE331 Computer Networks are strict prerequisite for this course. If you have not gone through these courses, you will be dropped from the class.

Reference books:

There is no fixed text for this course. However, there are some recommended books that will be followed in the class:

i. *Dreamweaver CS4* The missing manual
 McFarland, ISBN-9780596522926
ii. JavaScript Unleashed
 - Richard Wagner and R. Allen Wyke, Techmedia
iii. Internet and World Wide Web How to Program
 4th edition; Deitel & Deitel
iv. Beginning PHP 5, wrox press, 2004
 Wankyu Choi, Allan Kent, Chris Lea, Ganesh Presad, Chris Ullman
v. PHP5 and MySQL Bible
 - Tim Converse and Joyce Park with Clark Morgan (Wiley 2004)
vi. Advanced Java 2 Platform How to Program, 2nd edition (JDBC, *Servlet and JSP*)
 Deitel & Deitel

Tentative Course Schedule: The following course schedule is tentative and will be adjusted as needed to keep the course flexible and cover the most material.

Lecture #	Topic
1	Introduction to the course, Handout
2	Tools and Techniques for Data Intensive Web Application (DIWA)
3	XHTML Part I, II, Review of Links, Images and Tables
4	Dreamweaver CS4 Guided Tour; CSS
5	Quiz # 1; Project Description
6	Introduction to JavaScript, jQuery, AJAX

7	JavaScript Event Handing
8	Web Forms ; JavaScript Form Validation Techniques
9	Quiz # 2; DHTML, Spry Menu Bar
10	*Mid Term Exam*
11	Installing, configuring and testing Apache, MySQL and PHP (XAMPP, phpMyAdmin) configuring and testing Apache
12	Introduction to PHP; Handling Clients Data, File Handling, Uploading, Cookies, Sessions etc.
13	Project Technical Requirement Check List
14	Introduction to MySQL
15	PHP-MySQL Database Connectivity
16	Quiz#3
17	Generic Databases, SQL Queries, Divide Operation
18	Chapter 22: Getting Started with Dynamic Web Sites
19	Chapter 23: Adding Dynamic Data to your Pages
20	Chapter 24: Web Pages That Manipulate Database Records
21	Final Exam review class

Grading

Class Attendance	5%
Quizzes (4)	15%
Homework Assignment (3)	15%
Lab Exam (I)	5%
Mid Term Exam (I)	20%
Final Exam	20%
Term Project	20% (in a group of 3 student)

Grading Scale:

93 and above	A
90-92	A-
87-89	B+
83-86	B
80-82	B-
77-79	C+
73-76	C
70-72	C-
67-69	D+
60-66	D
Below 60	F

Projects:

There will be projects assigned throughout the semester. Each project will incorporate specific elements learned throughout the course. Students will have a limited amount of time to complete these projects and turn in complete code, documentation, and anything else outlined in the project write-up. Like assignments, no late projects will be accepted.

Attendance: Marks in attendance will be given according the following list.

Absent	**Marks**
0, 1	5
2, 3	4
4, 5	3
Other wise	0

CSC311/ETE335
Database Management Systems
Fall 2011

Department of Electrical Engineering and Computer Science (EECS)

North South University

Instructor: Dr. Emdad Ahmed
Email: emdad@northsouth.edu
Tel. 8852000 ext 1535
Meeting time: MW 1:00-2:30
Office Hour: MW 9:00-10:30
Meeting Place: SAC311
UGA: Md. Jahidul Islam (jahid1081@gmail.com)

Objective:

- As a first course on Database, extensively study of ER model
- Ability to Design relational Database System which is efficient and effective in terms of storage requirement, avoiding data redundancy and inconsistency
- Study of PL/SQL as relational database language
- Overview of emerging Internet Database technology like Web based system, HTML, XML etc.

Course Description (from Catalogue 2009-2010)

Examines the logical organization of databases. The entity-relationship model, the hierarchical, network, and relational data models and their languages. Functional dependencies and normal forms. Design, implement, and optimization of query languages; security and integrity; concurrency control, and distributed database systems. Prerequisite CSE225. 3 credits.

Text and References:

i. Fundamentals of Database Systems (5th edition)
   Ramez Elmarsi & Shamkant B. Navathe
ii. Database Management Systems (2nd Edition)
   Raghu Ramakrisnan & Johannes Gehrke
iii. Avi Silberschatz, Henry Korth and S. Sudarshan, Database System Concepts (Fifth Edition or later), McGraw-Hill.
iv. Michael Kifer, Arthur Bernstein and Philip Lewis, *Database Systems —An Application Oriented Approach*, 2nd Edition. Addison Wesley, 2005.
v. J.D. Ullman, Principles of Database and Knowledge-Base Systems, Computer Science Press, MD, 1988.
vi, D. Maier, The Theory of Relational Databases, Computer Science Press, MD, 1983

Topics to be covered (Tentative)

Introduction (Databases and Database users)
E-R model (relationship, sets, Keys); ER to relational mapping
Relational Algebra
Record Storage and Primary File Organization
Index Structures for Files; Hashing
SQL; PL/SQL
Functional Dependency and Normalization
Relational Database Design
Query Processing and Optimization
Transaction Processing
Concurrency Control Techniques
Internet Databases (HTML, Java Servlet, XML etc)

Grading:

i. Midterm I: 25%
ii. Quizzes: 10%
iii. Weekly Exercises (4): 10%
iv. Project: 15% (*in a group of 3 student*)
v. Class participation: 5%
vi. Final: 35%

Assignments:

There will be 4 weekly paper based theoretical assignment. Project assignment will consist of 3 parts:

i. Designing the ER model and ER to relational mapping (first part, due week 4)
ii. Constructing SQL queries and writing PL/SQL procedure (second part, due week 7)
iii. Constructing front end GUI, forms, report etc (third part, due week 10) Implementation Projects using .NET framework

CSE225
Data Structures and Algorithms

Department of Electrical Engineering and Computer Science (EECS)

North South University
Fall 2011

Instructor: Dr. Emdad Ahmed
Email: emdad@northsouth.edu
Office: SAC 922
Phone: 8852000 ext 1535
Class Hours: ST 9:40-11:10 (meets at SAC305) [section 1]
ST 11:20-12:50 (meets at SAC305) [section 2]
Lab Hours: ST 1:00-2:30 (meets at SAC513) [section 1]
ST 2:40-4:10 (meets at SAC513) [section 2]
Office Hours: ST 9:00-9:30; 4:10-5:00
GA/UGA: Saami Rahman (saamirahman@gmail.com)

Course Objectives

The course begins with core computer science concepts and moves into data structures. OOD methodology is stressed, as are searching and sorting algorithms, and basic coverage of abstract classes. Each new concept is introduced with complete programming examples, extensive exercise sets, and clear visual diagrams.

- Discuss and define abstract data types, encapsulation, information hiding and the fundamental differences between object oriented
- Implement common algorithms such as search for a particular data item, sort data, traverse through items in a data structure
- Discuss the properties and representation of elementary data structures such as stacks, queues, lists, and linked lists. Implement these data structures in C++
- Discuss the properties and representation of binary trees. Implement binary Trees in C++.
- Discuss and implement binary search trees (properties and operations)
- Discuss the properties and representation of graphs. Implement graphs in C++
- Graph algorithms such as breadth-first search and depth-first search of graphs will also be discussed.

Course Description: (*From Catalog 2009-2010*)

An introduction to the theory and practice of data structuring techniques. Topics include internal data representation, abstract data types, stacks, queues, list structures, recursive data structures, graphs and networks. Concept of object orientation as a data abstraction technique will be introduced. Prerequisite: CSE135. 4 credits (Theory 3 + Lab 1 credit).

Prerequisite: knowledge of C or C++ programming. Introduction to problem solving methods and algorithm development; data abstraction for structures such as stacks, queues, linked lists, trees, and graphs; searching and sorting algorithms and their analysis.

Text and references

- Data Structures and Algorithm Analysis in C++, Third Edition; Mark Allen Weiss
- Malik, D. S. C++ Programming: Program Design including Data Structures, Third edition.

  Scholl, Judy. Lab Manual for C++ Programming: From Program Analysis to Program Design. Textbooks are bundled with ISBN: 1423970136.
- Dietel, H and Dietel, P. C++ How to program, 6/E, Prentice Hall. ISBN 0136152503

Topics to be covered (tentative)

Topics covered will be chosen from the following:
Specific topic coverage includes:

- An Overview of Computers and Programming Languages
- Basic Elements of C++; I/O
- Control Structures I (Selection); Control Structures II (Repetition)
- User-Defined Functions I; User-Defined Functions II
- User-Defined Simple Data Types, Namespaces, and the string Type
- Arrays and Strings; Records (structs)
- Classes and Data Abstraction
- Inheritance and Composition
- Pointers, Classes, Virtual Functions, Abstract Classes, and Lists
- Overloading and Templates
- Exception Handling
- Recursion
- Linked Lists
- Stacks and Queues
- Searching and Sorting Algorithms
- Hashing
- Binary Trees
- Graphs

Course Grading:

Attendance	5%
Quizzes	40%
Mid Term Exam	25%
Final	30%

LAB Grading:

Attendance	20%
Programming Assignment	60%
LAB Exam	20%

Required Resources:

- Access to a computer
- Microsoft Visual Studio 2010 (available free of cost through MSDNAA)

Tentative Schedule

- Introduction to the course, Handout;
- Introduction to Visual Studio.NET 2010
- Programming Assignment # 1 hand out
- Linked Lists; Programming Assignment # 2 hand out
- Stacks and Queues
- Inheritance & composition, Programming Assignment # 3 hand out
- **Mid Term Exam**
- Recursion
- Searching and Sorting Algorithms
- Hashing
- Programming Assignment # 4 hand out
- Quiz # 3
- Binary Trees (In, Pre and Post order traversal)
- Programming Assignment # 5 hand out
- Graphs (BFS, DFS)
- Quiz # 4
- **Revision Class**
- **Final Exam**

CSE326 Compiler Construction

Department of Electrical Engineering and Computer Science (EECS)

North South University
Summer 2011

Instructor: Dr. Emdad Ahmed
Email: emdad@northsouth.edu
Office: SAC 922
Phone: 8852000 ext 1535
Meeting Place: SAC313
Class Hours: MW 1:00-2:30
Office Hours: MW 11:20-12:50
GA/UGA: Md. Jahidul Islam (jahid1081@gmail.com)

Course Objectives

A compiler is one of the most vital parts of a computer's system software, translating programs written in a high-level language into low-level commands that the machine can understand and execute. In this course you will implement a compiler that will take source code of a language and will generate assembly code. The project is a semester long project and throughout the project you will gain knowledge of how each part of a compiler works and how to implement one. We will be using C/C++ as our implementation language and tools like *lex* and *yacc* will be used.

Course Description:

(*From Catalog 2009-2010*) Compiler structure; lexical analysis, syntax analysis grammars, description of programming languages, automatically constructed recognizers and error recovery; and semantic analysis, semantic languages, semantic processes, intermediate language, optimization techniques, and extendible compilers. Prerequisite: CSE232 and CSE273. 3 credits.

Text and references

- Modern Compiler Design, John Wiley 2000
  - Dick Grune, Henri E. Bal, Cerial J.H. Jacobs and G. Langendoen
- Compilers Principles, Techniques, and Tools (2006)
  - Alfred V. Aho and Ullman
- Compiler Design
  - Reinhard Wilhelm, Dieter Maurer
- Advanced Compiler Design Implementation
  - Steven S. Muchnick

Topics to be covered (tentative)

- Introduction to Compiling
- Simple one pass compiler
- Lexical Analysis
- Syntax analysis
- Syntax-Directed Translation
- Abstract Syntax Tree (AST)
- Shift Reduce Parser, Top Down Parser, Bottom-Up Parser
- Type Checking
- Run time environments
- Intermediate code generation, code generation and optimization

Grading:

Attendance	5%
Programming Assignment	30%
Quizzes	15%
Mid Term Exam	20%
Final	30%

CSE325/CSE425
Programming Language Principles

Department of Electrical Engineering and Computer Science (EECS)

North South University
Summer 2011

Instructor: Dr. Emdad Ahmed
Email: emdad@northsouth.edu
Office: SAC 922
Phone: 8852000 ext 1535
Meeting Place: SAC311
Class Hours: MW 9:40-11:10
Office Hours: MW 11:20-12:50
GA/UGA: Saad Abdullah (*saad_a@yahoo.com*)

Course Objectives

- Provide an overview of the key paradigms used in developing modern programming languages
- Highlight several languages, viz. Python, C#, Prolog, which provide those features
- Provide sufficient formal theory to show where programming language design fits within the general computer science research agenda

Course Description:

(*From Catalog 2009-2010*) An introduction to the structure of programming languages. Formal specification of syntax and semantics; structure of algorithmic, list processing, string manipulation, data description, and simulation languages: basic data types, operations, statement types, and program structure; macro language and their implementation; and run time representation of programs and data. Prerequisite: CSE225. 3 credits.

This course covers the fundamental concepts of programming languages by discussing the design issues of the various language constructs, examining the design choices for these constructs in some of the most common languages, and critically comparing design alternatives. Procedural and functional programming will be introduced by C programming Language. Object oriented programming examples will be drawn from C++ and Java. Prolog will provide discussion of different programming paradigms. For the first time, we will extensively use Python as one of the most powerful programming language to date.

Text and references

- Concepts of Programming Languages, 8th Edition 2000, Robert W. Sebesta
- Programming Languages Design and Implementation, 4th edition, Prentice Hall 2001
  Terrence W. Pratt, Marvin V. Zelkowitz
- Programming Language Concepts, 3rd edition, John Wiley and sons
    - Carlo Ghezzi and Mehdi Jazayeri
- Programming Languages Concepts and Constructs, Addison Wesley by Ravi Sethi
- Programming Language Pragmatics, Michael L. Scott

Topics to be covered (tentative)

- Background of programming language techniques
- Names, Bindings, Type checking and scopes
- Primitive and reference data types and its specifications
- Concepts and issues related to different programming paradigm
- Language translation issues
- Describing syntax and semantics
- Parameter passing and side effects (call by value, call by reference)
- Functional, Logic and Rule Based programming languages

- Object Oriented Languages (encapsulation, inheritance, polymorphism etc)
- User defined ordinal data types specification
- Fixed and variable length record specification and implementations
- Pointer. List and File specification and implementations
- Sub program call return structure and implementations
- Namespaces, Packages
- Single and Multiple Inheritance, interface

Grading:

Attendance	5%
Programming Assignment	20%
Quizzes	15%
Mid Term Exam	30%
Final	30%

CSCI 120
Programming with Visual Basic II

Credits: 4
Instructor: Emdad Ahmed, *emdadahmed@hotmail.com*
Montana State University-Billings, College of Technology
3803 Central Avenue
Billings MT 59102
(406) 247-3082
Meeting Time: MWF 9:10-10:40 @COT BO42
Office: B043 at the COT campus
Office hours: Posted on office door of B043. Please make an appointment ahead of time if possible.

Office: B-43 College of Technology
Phone: 406-247-3082
E-mail: *emdadahmed@hotmail.com*
FAX: 406-652-1729
Office hours: Posted on office door, please make an appointment in advance.

Course Description

Explores advanced programming topics using Visual Basic .NET as a programming platform. Topics will include the creation of advanced Graphical User Interfaces, working with advanced data structures, network programming and use of ADO .NET for database interface.

Prerequisites

Math 121—Finite Mathematics

Books & Supplies

Books Required:

Richard Johnson, Diane Zak, Microsoft Visual Basic 2005: RELOADED, Advanced. Course Technology Incorporated, 2007, ISBN: 1-4188-3643-5 © 2007.ISBN-13: 978-1-4188-3643-6

Supplies:

Student Media: 1 USB drive required for course related files

Learning Outcomes:

This course provides an in depth study of advanced Visual Basic topics such as object-orientation, input/output, exception handling, database operations, Web site development and ADO.NET. The following are specific learning outcomes for students in the course.

- Be able to design object-oriented (OO) classes that are encapsulated, extendable and testable
- Understand how to use Inheritance and Polymorphism in OO languages
- Incorporate input validation, error handling and exception handling in programs
- Be able to design and create user-friendly Windows forms for user interaction
- Be able to create relational databases and use SQL for database operations
- Understand how to use the VB ADO.NET platform for data access and operations
- Understand and be able to create ASP.NET pages
- Understand XML and Web Services
- Be able to understand and appropriately implement Arrays, Collections and Generics
- Be able to prepare and present technical material

Course Requirement

Reading: There will be occasional reading assignments. Required reading should be completed before class in order to discuss the material during class periods.

Participation: Class activities will require active participation as individuals and groups. Participation is an integral component of this course. You are expected to attend regularly and to participate in class activities. These activities are sometimes graded and therefore missing class may have a negative effect on your grade.

Assignments: This course requires that you produce assignments of various types. Assignments may be turned in during class or via e-mail. Assignments are due at the end of the class on the due date given. Assignments turned in after the due date will be considered late and will not be accepted at the discretion of the instructor.

Extra Credit: At the instructor's discretion there may be opportunities provided for students to complete Extra Credit depending on class participation or extra assignments.

Exams: There will be a Midterm and Final Exam.

Quizzes: To promote informed discussions and to check understanding, quizzes over reading and lecture material may be given. Quizzes may or may not be announced and cannot be made up.

Oral Presentations

You may be required to make oral presentations of projects or code.

Grading:

Course grades will be made up of the following:

50%—Homework assignments, quizzes, projects and **classroom participation**.
25%—Midterm Test—Essay answer test combined with a project.
25%—Final Test—Cumulative essay answer test and cumulative project.

Grading Scale:

The following standard grading scale will be used:
A = 90-100% (superior)
B = 80-89% (above average)
C = 70-79% (average)
D = 60-69% (below average)
F = 59% or less (unacceptable)

Tentative Course Schedule: The following course schedule is tentative and will be adjusted as needed to keep the course flexible and cover the most material.

WEEK	COURSE MATERIAL	Chapter
1	Reviewing Microsoft Visual Basic 2005 Reloaded: Part 1	Chapter 1
2	Reviewing Microsoft Visual Basic 2005 Reloaded: Part 2	Chapter 2
3	Objects and Classes	Chapter 3
4	Object Orientation: Inheritance and Polymorphism	Chapter 4
5	Input Validation, Error Handling, and Exception Handling	Chapter 5
6	More about Windows Forms	Chapter 6
7	More about Windows Forms cont	Chapter 6
8	***MIDTERM REVIEW AND EXAM***	
9	Relational Databases and SQL	Chapter 7
10	Accessing Data with ADO.NET	Chapter 8
11	An Introduction to ASP.NET	Chapter 9
12	More ASP.NET: Database, XML, and Web Services	Chapter 10
13	Arrays, Collections, and Generics	Chapter 11
14	Multithreading in Visual Basic	Chapter 12
15	***FINAL EXAM***	

Course Policies and Comments:

In order to make our class a comfortable and encouraging learning environment for everyone, all students are expected to abide by the following policies:

- Be on-time for class. If you are late, enter as quietly as possible.
- Find out what you missed from another student after the missed class period.
- Listen when others are speaking; keep extraneous conversations to a minimum.
- Treat your classmates, instructors, and guests with respect, courtesy and integrity.
- **During lectures or class discussions please participate or listen respectfully and do not be surfing the Internet.**

Drug Free Schools: In accordance with the Drug-Free Schools and Communities Act of 1989, the unlawful possession, use, or distribution of alcohol and illicit drugs by Montana State University Billings employees and its students on institutional property or at any of its activities is prohibited. Communications with others including discussion areas and email will be done in a professional, courteous, and polite manner. Affirmative Action: Inquiries regarding application of these and other regulations should be directed to either the College's Affirmative Action Office, Montana Office of Civil Rights, Montana Department of Education, Helena, Montana; or to the Office of Federal Contract Compliance Programs, Department of Labour, Dallas, Texas. Equal Opportunity: It is the policy of MSU-Billings to provide equal educational opportunity and employment opportunities and to provide service benefits to all students and employees without regard to race, colour, religion, national origin, sex, age, disability or any other status or characteristic protected by applicable state of federal law.

Academic Honesty: Cheating, plagiarism, and other acts of academic dishonesty are regarded as serious offenses. Instructors have the responsibility to submit, in a written report to the Associate Vice President of Student Life, any such incident that cannot be resolved between the instructor and student. Depending on the nature of the offense, serious penalties may be imposed, ranging from loss of points to expulsion from the class or college. Student rights and responsibilities can be located in the MSU-Billings Student Handbook. It is expected that all course work will be your original work. Evidence of cheating or plagiarism will be grounds for disciplinary action (see Student Handbook). Infractions of the code of Student Conduct will be handled as described in the Current Student Handbook.

Attendance: Satisfactory completion of this course requires regular and consistent class attendance as well as active participation. I expect you to be punctual and to attend class regularly. If you must arrive late, please try to be as quiet as possible to avoid disrupting the class. If you cannot attend class for any reason, you are responsible for finding out from a classmate what you have missed.

Available Support Services

Library

To find materials, you will want to familiarize yourself with the MSU-Billings, COT library. In addition to the library here, your student fees also gain you access to the library on the main campus. You will need your student ID card for the college libraries. The MSU-Billings library Web site is *http://www.msubillings.edu/library/.*To access the MSU-B Web site from home, follow the instructions for "Off-Campus Access" on the library home page.

Academic Support Center

Free tutoring services for students are available in the Academic Support Center at the COT, A035, Monday through Thursday, 8 a.m.-6 p.m. and Friday, 8 a.m.-5 p.m. The Academic Support Center on the senior campus is open from 8 a.m.-7 p.m. Monday through Thursday, 8 a.m.-5 p.m. Friday, and 9 a.m.—noon Saturday. Tutors are available to assist students with math, writing, reading, anatomy and physiology, and other specialty areas for specific majors. See http://www.msubillings.edu/asc/ for more information or call 247-3022 (COT) or 657-1641 (senior campus). Tutoring services are available through the Academic Support Center, A035, Monday through Friday, 8 a.m.-5 p.m. not only for this class, but also for math and other courses.

Disability Support Center

Students with disabilities, whether physical, learning, or psychological, who believe that they may need accommodations in this class, are encouraged to contact Disability Support Services as soon as possible to ensure that such accommodations are implemented in a timely fashion. Please contact DSS to verify your eligibility for any classroom accommodations and for academic assistance related to your disability by calling 657-2283. The DSS contact person at the College of Technology is Kelley Williford, room A071. She is available Monday-Friday, 9 a.m.-2 p.m. Disability-related information is confidential, falling under medical information, Title V of the Rehabilitation Act of 1973.

CSC2000
Introduction to C++ Programming
Winter 2007

Department of Computer Science

Wayne State University

Instructor: Emdad Ahmed
Email: emdad@wayne.edu
Office Hour: Tuesday 6:30-7:30 State Hall 308
Office Tel: 313-577-5604
Meeting time: Tuesday 7:30-9:20pm
Meeting Place: State Hall 218
LAB Instructor for section 1: Md. Shazzad Hosain
Email: shazzad@wayne.edu
LAB Instructor for section 3: Yong Xi
Email: yongxi@wayne.edu
LAB Hour: Thursday 7:30-9:20 (State Hall 313) [section 1]
Thursday 7:30-9:20 (State Hall 314) [section 3]

Course Description

This course is an introductory study in object orientated programming using C++. Students will learn the basics of the C++ programming language and how to design programs using object orientated programming (OOP). At the end of the course you should be able to develop C++ programs using OOP.

Textbook: C++ How to Program, 5[th]Edition
Deitel and Deitel ISBN: 0-13-185757-6 Prentice Hall, 2006

Programming Assignments

Homework assignments have to be turned in on the due date. Assignments received by the beginning of the class on the due date will be considered as on time. No homework assignments will be accepted past the submission deadline.

Programming Assignment #	To be assigned	Due
1	Jan 16	Jan 25
2	Jan 23	Feb 1
3	Jan 30	Feb 8
4	Feb 6	Feb 15
5	Feb 13	Feb 22
6	Feb 20	Mar 1
7	Feb 27	Mar 8
8	Mar 20	Mar 29
9	Mar 27	Apr 5
10	Apr 3	Apr 19

Grading

Mid term	20%
LAB Attendance	10%
Programming Assignments (10)	40%
Final	30%

CSC1500
Fundamental Structures of Computer Science
Spring/Summer 2006

Department of Computer Science

Wayne State University

Instructor: Emdad Ahmed
Email: emdad@wayne.edu
Tel: 313-577-5604
Meeting time: MW 5:30-7:10
Meeting Place: State Hall 111
Office Hour: MW 4:30-5:30 State Hall 308

Course Description

This course introduces to the fundamental discrete structures of computer science. This course can be used to satisfy the Computer Literacy Requirement. The goal of this course is to introduce students to ideas and techniques from discrete mathematics that are widely used in Computer Science. The course aims to present these ideas "in action"; each one will be geared towards a specific significant application. Thus, students will see the purpose of the techniques at the same time as learning about them.

Course Objectives

Logic and mathematics are powerful tools in the study of computer science. While programming languages fall in and out of flavor with the passage of time, formal reasoning and mathematical techniques can always be used in the analysis of programming problems and solutions. This course introduces students to propositional logic and first-order logic-reasoning frameworks that have varied applications including integrated circuit design, artificial intelligence and algorithm correctness. Mathematical techniques such as recurrence relations and order of growth analysis will be taught as precursors to the analysis and comparison of algorithms. Further tools, such as combinatorial principles and probability will serve to complement this. Two of the most common data structures in computer science, trees and graphs, will have their properties examined from a mathematical viewpoint. By the end of this course, the successful student will understand and be able to apply the following concepts:

- Propositions, truth tables, logical equivalences, predicates, quantifiers
- Proofs, inference rules, valid arguments
- Sets, set operations, functions
- Algorithms, growth functions, big-O notation, algorithm complexity
- Algorithms, growth functions, big-O notation, algorithm complexity
- Integers, integer division, applications of number theory, matrices
- Sequences, summations, cardinality, mathematical induction
- Recursive definitions, structural induction, recursive algorithms
- Relations, closures, equivalence relations, partial orderings
- Counting principles, pigeonhole principle, inclusion and exclusion principles
- Permutations, combinations, binomial coefficients
- Discrete probability, probability theory, expected values, variance

Textbook: Discrete Mathematics and Its Applications, Kenneth H. Rosen, 5th Edition

Tentative Schedule

Lecture #	**Date**	**Topic**
1	May 8	Introduction to the course, Handout
2	Mat 10	The Fundamentals of Logic
3	May 15	Basic Proof Methods
4	May 17	Theory of Sets
5	May 22	Functions
6	May 24	Algorithms
7	May 29	Orders of Growth, Algorithmic Complexity
8	May 31	Basic Number Theory, Applications of Number Theory
9	June 5	Matrices
10	June 7	Proof Strategies
11	June 12	Sequences, Summations
12	*June 14*	Mathematical induction, Inductive Proofs
13	June 19	***Mid Term Exam***
14	June 21	Recursion
15	June 26	Combinatorics, Binomial Coefficients
16	June 28	Probability Theory, distribution
17	July 3	Random Variable, Expected value and Variance
18	July 5	Recurrence Relations I
19	July 10	Recurrence Relations II
20	July 12	Relations
21	July 17	Graph Theory I
22	July 19	Graph Theory II
23	July 24	Trees
24	July 26	*Revision class*
25	July 31	**Final Exam**

Homework Assignments

Homework assignments have to be turned in on the due date. Assignments received by the beginning of the class on the due date will be considered as on time. No homework assignments will be accepted past the submission deadline.

Grading

Mid term	30%
Howe works (8)	40%
Final	30%

CSC348
Artificial Intelligence
Fall 2005

Department of Computer Science & Engineering

North South University

Lecturer: Emdad Ahmed
Email: emdad@northsouth.edu **Tel.** 9885611-20 ext 187
Meeting time: ST 2:40-4:10
Lab Hours: TBA
Meeting Place: STR1135
Lab Instructor: Humayun K. Islam
Teaching Assistant: TBA

Overview

This course should provide students with a foundation in the basic theory and programming techniques of Artificial Intelligence (AI). These will be motivated by an introduction to a variety of application areas.

Artificial intelligence is the basic discipline underpinning all "smart" systems—e.g., smart Internet applications, smart e-commerce systems. Most complicated search problems cannot be tackled directly using complete search procedures, as completed searches tend to take millions of years to terminate, even on current generation computers. Consequently it is necessary to use heuristic algorithms that estimate the part of the search space most likely to yield useful results, and "prune" the rest. Heuristic algorithms are part of the domain of AI.

AI also includes techniques for specialized areas, including machine learning, natural language understanding/processing, computer vision, robotics and computer game playing.

Course Objectives

This subject will provide students with the basic concepts, theory and techniques of Artificial Intelligence.

By the end of the session, students should:

- have an understanding of a variety of **knowledge representation** (*the study of how to put knowledge into a form that a computer can reason with*) and computer Inference, heuristic programming techniques, including:
    - frames and semantic networks
    - search methods
    - use of predicate logic for representing knowledge
    - planning
    - reasoning under uncertainty
- be able to analyze an AI problem in terms of these methods
- have a working knowledge of a common AI programming language: Prolog, and understand the relationship between logic and Prolog

Textbook:

Russell, S. and Norvig, P., Artificial Intelligence: A Modern Approach, Second edition, Pearson Education, 2003.

References:

Bratko, I. (2001). *PROLOG Programming for Artificial Intelligence* Addison-Wesley

Tentative Schedule

Lecture #	Topic
1	Introduction to the course, Handout
2	Introduction to AI
3	Problem solving and Search (problem types, formulation, example problems, basic Search algorithms)
4	Informed Search Strategies (Best First, Greedy, A*, Heuristics search)
5	Quiz # 1
6	Introduction to Prolog, Part I
7	Other Searching Techniques
8	Knowledge and Reasoning (propositional Logic, predicate Logic)
9	Introduction to Prolog, Part II
10	Introduction to Prolog, Part III
11	Quiz # 2
12	*Mid Term Exam (29th October Saturday)*
13	Logic Grammars, BNF Notation; DCG; Context Dependence; Parse Trees
14	Natural Language Processing
15	Prolog Programming Assignment on NLP
16	Quiz # 3
17	Semantic Networks and Frames
18	Bottom-Up Chart Parsing
19	Uncertain Reasoning
20	Induction of Decision Trees
21	Robotics & Computer Vision, Java Programming Assignment on Computer Vision
22	Revision, Final Exam Question discussion
23	Project Presentation
24	Quiz # 4

Grading

Mid term I	*20%*
Prolog Programming Assignment (3)	15%
Java Programming Assignment (1)	5%
Class Participation	5%
Quizzes (4)	15%
Term Project	10% (in a group of 3 student)
Final	30%

CSE338 /ETE331
Computer Networks
Fall 2005

Department of Computer Science & Engineering

North South University

Lecturer: Emdad Ahmed
Email: emdad@northsouth.edu **Tel.** 9885611-20 ext 187
Meeting time: ST 9:40-11:10 **Lab Hours: TBA**
Meeting Place: STR201
Lab Instructor: Humayun K. Islam **Teaching Assistant**: TBA

Course Objectives

There are two goals of this course: to examine in detail the fundamentals of protocols used to implement networks; and to examine how these principles are used in practice on successful networks, with emphasis on the use of the TCP/IP suite of protocols in the global Internet.

- To help students gain a general understanding of the principles and concepts governing the operations of computer networks
- To provide the students with the opportunity to become skillful in implementation and use of communication protocols.

Course Description

This course is intended for students with no background in data communications. This course covers the fundamentals of data communications and their application in modern data networks, with particular emphasis on the Internet. Topics include: the general organization of computer networks, data transmission, point-point links, multi-point links and media access, packet switching, internetworking, end-end protocols (transport and application), congestion control and resource allocation, compression and other data manipulation, security, and an overview of applications.

The following is a list of the major topics covered in this subject:

- Introduction to Networks, Internet Architecture, Access Systems, protocol layers
- Application Layer Overview: HTTP, FTP, SMTP, DNS Protocols, Content Distribution Network (CDN)
- Introduction to Socket Programming with TCP and UDP, Transport Layer, Reliable and Unreliable data transfer, Congestion and Flow Control
- Network Layer and Routing Protocols (Distance Vector, link state etc.)
- IPv4, ICMP, Internet Routing Protocols, Multicasting, Mobile IP
- Link Layer Protocols, Error Detection and Error Correction Techniques, CRC
- High Speed Digital Access: DSL, Cable Modems
- Local Area Networks, Ethernet, Token Ring, Fast Ethernet, VLAN, Hub, Bridge and Switches
- Wireless and Mobile Networks: Wi-Fi 802.11, Cellular Internet Access
- Multimedia Networking: RTP, RTSP, RTCP, RSVP, SIP, Integrated Services and Differentiated Services
- Access Control: Firewalls

Textbook:

i. Computer Networking—A Top-Down Approach Featuring the Internet, J. Kurose and K. Ross, Addition Wesley, 3rd Ed. 2005

References:

a. Behrouz A. Forouzan, Data Communications and Networking, 3rd Edition 2003, Tata MGH.
b. Java Network Programming, 3rd edition 2004, Elliotte Rusty Harold, Oreilly
c. Computer Networks, Prentice Hall PTR; ISBN: 0133499456; 4th edition, Tanenbaum
d. Peterson, Larry L., and Davie, Bruce S. Computer Networks: A Systems Approach, 3rd edition. Morgan Kaufmann, 2003. ISBN 1-55860-832-X or 1-55860-833-8.
e. Computer Networks and Internets, with Internet Applications by *Douglas E. Comer, Ralph E. Droms*; Prentice Hall; ISBN: 0130914495; 4th edition, 2004

Tentative Schedule

Lecture #	**Topic**
1	Introduction to the course, Handout
2	Chapter 1 Computer Networks and Internet
3	Chapter 1 continued
4	Chapter 2 Application Layer
5	Introduction to Socket Programming
6	Quiz # 1
7	Chapter 2 continued
8	Chapter 3 Transport Layer
9	Chapter 3 continued, QoS
10	Revision of Chapter 1, 2, 3
11	Quiz # 2
12	*Mid Term Exam (29th October Saturday)*
13	Introduction to Ethereal Labs
14	Chapter 4 Network Layer
15	Chapter 4 continued
16	Chapter 5 Link Layer and LAN
17	Chapter 5 continued

18	Quiz # 3
19	Chapter 6 Wireless and Mobile Networks
20	Chapter 6 continued
21	Firewalls,
22	Revision of chapter 4, 5, 6
23	Theoretical Project Presentation
24	Quiz # 4

Grading

Mid term I	20%
Programming Assignment (2)	10%
Hands on Practical Assignment (1)	5% (in a group of 3 student)
LAB Exam	5%
Class Participation	5%
Quizzes (4)	20%
Theoretical Project	10% (in a group of 3 student)
Final	25%

CSC 497
Advanced Computer Networks
Summer 2002

Department of Computer Science

North South University

Lecturer: Emdad Ahmed
Email: emdad@northsouth.edu
Tel. 9885611 ext 187
Meeting time: MW 9:40-11:10
Meeting Place: STR 201
Teaching Assistant: TBA

Text:

Internetworking with TCP/IP Principles, Protocols, and Architectures (Fourth Edition 2000)
- Douglas E. Comer

References:

i. An Engineering Approach to Computer Networking
   - S. Keshav
ii. UNIX Network programming
   - Stevens

iii. Gigabit Networks
- Paul Izzo

iv. Engineering Internet Quality of Service (QoS)
(Publisher Artech House, June 2002, USA)
- Sanjay Jha

Objectives:

1. Develop good understanding of Internet routing and switching architectures, protocols and algorithms
2. Gain in depth knowledge of switching fundamentals in ATM networks
3. Learn routing techniques for ATM-based Internets or IP over ATM networks
4. Understand multicasting techniques and routing algorithms for IP networks
5. Cover recent QoS related developments by IETF/IEEE such as: Intserv, Diffserv, RSVP and LAN QoS

Topics to be covered (Tentative)

This subject will focus on the routing and switching architectures, algorithms and protocols for packet switching networks, both connectionless and connection oriented networks. It will examine the fundamental concepts of routing and switching data in two widely deployed packet switching networks, the Internet and the ATM networks.

The emphasis of this subject will be on the standard and generic technologies for routing and switching. This subject will also cover the fundamentals of Quality of Service (QoS) based networks, with an emphasis on the next generation Internet architectures and protocols. Topics include scheduling policies (fair queuing, priority queuing etc.), congestion avoidance/control schemes (RED, RIO etc.), admission control, multimedia protocols (RTP, RTCP etc).

The following is a list of the major topics that will be covered in this subject:

Introduction:
Internet Addressing: CIDR, NAT, VPN. Chap 10, 20
Internet Routing: Chap 14, 15, 16
ATM Networks: Chap 18
Switching: Time-division, Space-division, Time-Space, Time-Space-Time, Multistage crossbar switching; Chap 8 of Keshav
IP Switching: Multi Protocol Label Switching (MPLS)

Internet Multicasting: Chap 17; Chap 11 of Keshav
Mobile IP: Chap 19.
ICMP: Chap 9
Review of Socket Programming in C
Introduction to QoS and Best Effort Network
Quality of Service Fundamentals
Packet Scheduling
Flow Control, Congestion Control and Queue Management (RED, RIO)
Integrated Services (IntServ) Architecture
Resource Reservation Protocols (RSVP)
QoS in LAN environment (IEEE 802.1p, Subnet Bandwidth Manager)
Differentiated Services (DiffServ) Architecture
Policy based Management
Student presentations on recent advances (mini-conference)

Grading:

Mid term I	20%
Assignment	25%
Quizzes	10%
Participation	5%
Mini-Conference	15% (in a group of 3 students)
Final	25%

Assignment:

There will be one theoretical assignment on BGP, NAT and OSPF, Programming Assignment (in C) to simulate distant vector routing algorithm); 4 lab exercises on client-server socket programming in C (in a group of 3 students)

CSC373
Design and Analysis of algorithm
Fall 2002

Department of Computer Science

North South University

Lecturer: Emdad Ahmed
Email: emdad@northsouth.edu
Tel. 9885611 ext 187
Meeting time: ST 1:00-2:30pm (section 1);
MW 11:20-12:50 (section 2)
Office Hours: 11:20 AM-1:00 PM (ST)
Meeting Place: STR 203 (section 1) STR 1235 (section 2)
Teaching Assistant: TBA

Objectives:

- To gain a comprehensive introduction to the modern study of computer science
- Familiarity with important algorithms and data structures
- Ability to design, evaluate running time, and prove correctness of algorithm
- To understand the implementation concerns, engineering issues and practical utility of the algorithms learned in the course

Text:

Introduction to Algorithms (Second Edition, MIT press 2001)
- Thomas H. Cormen, Charles E. Leiserson, and Ronald L. Rivest

References:

Fundamentals of Computer Algorithm
Horowitz and Sahni
The art of Computer Programming Vol 1, 2
- Donald K Knuth

Grading:

Mid term I:	15%
Mid term II:	15%
Assignment (3)	25%
Class Participation	5%
Quiz I:	5%
Quiz II:	5%
Final	30%

Syllabus:

- Introduction; Role of Algorithms in Computing
- Mathematical Foundation
    - Growth of function, Summations, Sets, Counting and Probability
- Solving Recurrences using
  Substitution, iteration and master method
- Sorting and Order Statistics
  Heap sort, Quick sort, Bubble sort, Insertion sort, Selection sort
- Horner's rule for evaluating polynomial
- Probabilistic analysis and Randomized Algorithms
- Sorting in Linear Time (Counting sort, Radix sort, Bucket sort)
- Data Structure
  Stacks, Queues, Hash Table, Binary Search Trees
- Dynamic Programming
  Matrix chain multiplication, longest common subsequence (LCS)
- Greedy Algorithm (Knapsack problem, Huffman codes)
- Amortized Analysis (aggregate method, accounting method, potential method)

- Graph Algorithm
  Representation of graph, BFS, DFS, MST, Dijkstra's shortest path algorithm
- Matrix Operations (Strassen's algorithm for matrix multiplication)
- Selected topics
  Number-Theoretic Algorithm (GCD, modular arithmetic, RSA, primarily testing)
  String Matching (Knuth-Morris-Pratt algorithm)
  NP-Completeness (Polynomial time, super polynomial time, polynomial time verification, NP-completeness and reducibility, NP-complete problems)

Assignment:

There will be 3 assignments for this course. 1st one on Maintaining Priority Queue using Heap Data structure; 2nd one on graph theoretic problem Dijkstra's shortest path algorithm, articulation point of a network etc. and the final one on number theoretic algorithm (implementing RSA algorithm on encryption/decryption). 3 weeks will be given for each programming problem to be solved.

CSC273
Theory of Computation
Summer 2003

Department of Computer Science & Engineering

North South University

Meeting Time: MW 9:40-11:10 **Meeting Place:** SPZ601
Lecturer: Emdad Ahmed
Phone: 9885611 ext 187 (office)
E-mail: emdad@northsouth.edu
Teaching Assistant: Saiful Islam

Text:

i. *Elements of the Theory of Computation,* by Harry R. Lewis and Christos H. Papadimitriou
ii. Introduction to Finite Automata, Languages and Computation
    By Hop croft, Motwani & Ullman
    Pearson Education, 2nd edition 2002
iii. Mechanical Theorem Proving (chapter 1, 2 and 3 only)
    - Chang

References:

Theory of Computation, by Derrick Wood

Course Description:

In this course we will discuss some of the fundamental mathematical ideas underlying computer science. We will focus on three related areas: **automata theory**, **computability theory**, and **computational complexity.**

Computability: primitive recursive functions, computable functions, universal programs, undecidability, Church-Turing thesis, Turing machines, recursively enumerable sets and elementary recursive function theory;

Complexity: the sets P and NP, NP-completeness and Cooks theorem. Logic: predicate logic and its unsatisfiability problem.

Automata theory examines the question "what is a computer?" and "what can it do?" We examine three fundamental mathematical models of computation (finite automata, pushdown automata, and Turing machines) and study their capabilities and limitations.

Computability theory is a natural extension of automata theory. It examines the question "what is the most powerful model of computation?" and "what can it do?" The answers turn out to be very surprising!

Complexity theory addresses the questions "how long does it take to solve a particular problem?" and "Is a particular problem solvable?" We study several complexity classes such as **P** and **NP** among others and develop some interesting results that relate these classes to one another.

Objectives:

By the end of this course students are expected to:

- use regular languages to express and recognize patterns
- to be able to construct mathematical models (FSA, DFA, PDA etc.) from a given language
- recognize tractable and intractable problems
- develop skill in proving theorems of theoretical computer science

Grading:

Students will be evaluated based on their performance in the exams and weekly assignments. There will be 2 midterms during the semester and one final exam. In addition there will be weekly homework assignments. The assignments are designed to enhance the students' understanding of the subject matter and prepare them for the exams. There will also be some points for class participation. The break up of the grading scheme will be as follows:

Midterm 1	20%
Midterm 2	20%
Final	30%
Quizzes	15%
Assignments	15%

CSC 135
Fundamentals of Computer Programming
Summer 2002

Department of Computer Science

North South University

Lecturer: Emdad Ahmed
Email: emdad@northsouth.edu
Tel. 9885611 ext 187
Meeting time: MW 11:20-12:50 (section 3)
1:00-2:30 (SECTION 3 LAB)
Meeting Place: SPZ631 (SECTION 3)
Teaching Assistant: TBA

Objective:

As a first course of programming, students will learn basic data types, I/O handling, class, sub-class, looping, switch, case, methods and signature, string tokenizer, object oriented programming, inheritance, interface, Java Applet, Swing package, GUI design, sorting, searching, Stack, Queue, Linked list data structure etc. By the end of semester, students are expected to learn and use a number of Java reference manual's API which will make life easier in later advanced level computer science courses.

Text:

i. Java software solutions, Foundation of Program Design
   - John Lewis & William Loftus
ii. Java How to Program [*specially for end of book chapter exercises, quiz questions*]
   - Deitel & Deitel

References:

i. Just JAVA
   - Peter van der LINDEN
ii. JAVA by example
   - Jerry R. Jackson; Alan L. McClellan
iii. Java in a Nutshell

Grading:

i. Mid term I: 15%
ii. Mid term II: 15%
iii. Quizzes: 10%
iv. Assignment (5-6): 25%
v. Class participation: 5%
vi. Final: 30%

Syllabus:

Computer Systems; Software Concepts; Program elements; Objects and classes; Graphics
Inheritance, Enhanced class design; Graphical User Interfaces, Introduction to Swing package
Recursion, Sorting and Searching; Advanced flow of control
Data Structure (Stack, Queue, Linked List) [chapter 22 of Deitel & Deitel]

Assignment:

End of book chapter exercise assignment will be given in each week as practice/grading. In addition to that some 3-4 large project assignment like parsing HTML document; 2D array processing; matrix operation (transpose, multiply); MouseMotionListener; ActionListener; creating interactive Java applet etc. will be given. Usually 2/3 weeks will be given to complete each assignment and no extension to deadline will be given. Students are expected to spend considerable amount of time in lab to work out the problems.

I had the opportunity to conduct Database Management Systems course for a number of times. I used to assign a semester long project for the students. Below the technical requirement of the project is specified.

CSC311/ETE335
Database Management Systems

Department of Electrical Engineering and Computer Science (EECS)

North South University (NSU)

Semester: Fall 2011
Instructor: Dr. Emdad Ahmed

Course Project
Draft Description

Consider designing a real estate database which keeps information about homes, appliances, agents, owners and locations in Bangladesh. Typical information kept in the database includes:

- ***Homes***: *FloorSpace, Floors, BedRooms, BathRooms, LandSize, YearConstructed.* Homes can be further categorized into mansions, apartments, townhomes and condos. They will have all the properties of a home, but they will have distinguishing properties from homes and from one another. For example, mansions must have more than 3,000 sqft of floor space and more than 1 acres land size, and apartments cannot have more than one floor. The set of such homes are distinct—no two homes will be simultaneously an apartment and a mansion, for example.

- ***Location***: A home can have an identification number and resides in a unique address. Notice that even though condos may have the same address, their unit number distinguishes them from each other. You need to account for this fact also. An address, on the other hand, while unique, its components may not. For example, a street may have several house, a city will have several streets, and several postal codes. No two streets have the same name within a postal code. A city will have a changing population.
- ***Appliances***: Appliances have a model name or number, year, a maker, a name and a price. Homes will include numerous appliances made by different manufacturers. Appliances are identified either by their model number, or by the make and the name of the appliance.
- ***Agents***: Agents are identified using a unique agent identity. Agents sell homes to different people called home owners. Agents sell the homes to an owner who will own the homes for some period of time, and can sell them to another person through an agent possibly at a different price. Two agents cannot sell the same home at the same time. Agents receive commission (percentage) on the purchase price of a home. The rate of commission is determined by the real estate company the agent works for. She/he is allowed to work for many different companies such that the company will have an office in the city he/she sells homes.
- ***Owners***: Home owners have a name, a unique national identification number, number of dependents (family members), income, age and a profession.

Design the database keeping in mind that users of this database may ask some of the following questions for a variety of reasons.

1. List all the homes owned by a given owner in a given city.
2. List all the homes that were sold more than once.
3. Find the most expensive home an owner ever bought.
4. Find all the homes that include all the appliances by the same maker.
5. Find owners who do not own the homes they used to own.
6. Find the total commissions earned by an agent. Assume that commission earned is on the purchased price of a home he/she sells.
7. Find people who own apartments as well as mansions.
8. List all the homes below a price in a given city.
9. List owners who own all the most expensive homes in a given city.
10. Find homes that up for sale in a given city that meet certain buyer choices such as number of bedrooms, baths, etc.

You also need to consider some of the following transactions:

1. Adding an agent into the database.
2. Adding a new home to the database.
3. Moving a home from available for sale list to the owned list.
4. Making a person a home owner and consistently changing all related information.

The implementation should preserve all ICs—including the FDs identified during the design process and the constraints involving definitions such as Program of Study, prerequisites, etc.

Design a conceptual scheme using entity relationship model and then develop the corresponding relational scheme in BCNF. If a BCNF scheme does not exist, then design a 3NF scheme. Implement all tables, constraints and queries using SQL. Design a user friendly interface for populating the tables, and execute the following pre-fabricated queries. Submit your reports on the ER diagram and the BCNF design as scheduled. Submit final report on the due date after you implemented your database. Schedule a demo time with your tutor before the final exam and during the demo period.

What you should do: *The deliverables*

Phase I: Based on the description and queries/transactions given above, develop an ER diagram for the conceptual scheme of a suitable database for the above application. Make appropriate choices for entities, relationships, attributes, etc. ***This is due Monday, October 31, 2011***.

Phase II: Convert the ER schema from Phase I into an equivalent relational schema. Identify all functional dependencies, compute all keys, show all foreign keys, and referential integrity constraints. Develop a relational schema conforming to Boyce-Codd Normal Form/Third Normal Form. ***This is due Monday, November 21, 2011***.

Phase III: Implement the database on Oracle. Implement the sample queries and transactions. You will receive bonus points for implementing additional non-trivial queries and transactions. Demonstrate your implementation with test data. ***Demonstrations will take place during the period December 5 through December 9, 2011***. You must schedule a time with your lab Instructor for your demonstration before December 1, 2011. ***The Phase III comprehensive project report is due on Monday, December 5, 2011***.

Important Notes

For all phases, you need to submit only one report per group. Write the identification for each member of the group on the cover page. You are allowed to submit handwritten reports. You are allowed to work in groups of 2 or 3. You should submit one final report for your group. It will include the E-R diagram, Relational schema, BCNF/3NF decomposition of the relational schema, implementation code, and sample executions of queries and transactions. Your project may not be a list of Oracle scripts which implement the queries and transactions. It should be similar to a commercial application with menus and interfaces.

Project Grading Scheme

1. Correct ER/relational design—10%.
2. Appropriate interface/forms design—20%.
3. Satisfactory implementation of queries—30%.
4. Satisfactory transaction implementation—20%.
5. Demonstration—10%.
6. Individual contributions—10%.
7. Project report—pass/fail. Must pass this component.

I had the opportunity to conduct a course *Internet and Web Technology* at NSU for 10 semesters. I would recommend anyone interested in Web programming to consult the *www.w3schools.com* site.

Information transmitted to the Web server in a Common Gateway Interface (CGI) request is fundamentally just a list of (name, value) pairs with an appropriate Uniform Resource Locator (URL) encoding string. Thus we can characterize a Web form with n controls as a tuple $F = \langle U, (N_1, V_1), (N_2, V_2), \ldots, (N_n, V_n) \rangle$, where U is the URL to which the encoded CGI request is sent and the (N_i, V_i) are (name, value) pairs to be sent. There are two ways to submit a form for CGI processing. HTTP POST method submits the form in the body of the request. HTTP GET method submits the form as part of the URL. A question mark (?) separates the base URL and action path from the encoded names and values. Writing the necessary behind-the-scenes processing software can be complex, but the concepts behind forms are straightforward:

1. First, someone fills out a form on your Web page, and then clicks the Submit button
2. Next, the Web browser transmits the form data over the Internet to a program on your Web server

3. The program collects the data and does something with it—whatever you and the programmer decide it should do: For example, send the data off as an email to you, search a vast database of information, or store the information in a database
4. Finally, the Web server returns a page to the Web visitor. It may be a standard Web page with a message like "Thanks for the info", or a page dynamically generated by the program itself—like a detailed invoice page, or the results of a search.

In the course, I used to assign a semester long project for the students. Below is the Project Technical Requirement Checklist.

CSC382/CSC482/ETE334 Internet and Web Technology

Department of Electrical Engineering and Computer Science (EECS)

North South University (NSU)
Fall 2011

Project Technical Requirement Checklist
Project Presentation Due: Monday, December 12, 2011

In this project you will apply all the tools/techniques that we have learned in the course CSC382/CSC482/ETE334, viz., XHTML, CSS, JavaScript, PHP, MySQL etc. Specifically you are required to implement a dynamic Web site backed by MySQL database. This is a group project consisting of 2-3 members. Strict deadline for project completion and presentation is Monday, December 12, 2011. Please remember that no extension will be granted. You will be using Dreamweaver CS4/CS5 and will test the dynamic Web site in *localhost* using XAMPP environment.

Here is the brief technical outline, regardless of any projects that you have been assigned to:

1. Choose a page format (most preferably 3 column fixed with header and footer)
2. Put all the contact info, company logo image in the header
3. Header should also contain a *Spry Menu Bar* (you are free to choose whatever you will add in the menu bar)

4. Left side bar should have a number of links (you are free to choose anything that might be interesting for the site)
5. Main content will display the most important piece of information of the page
6. Right side bar can be used for displaying images, banner advertisement etc
7. Footer should display copyright information, developed by you etc
8. Design a database consisting of 4-5 tables. One of the tables should contain registered users' information, their email, password etc. It is important to identify the PK and FK for all the tables
9. Populate the database with dummy data for testing purpose only
10. The dynamic Web site will be used for 2 types of user: admin and general user
11. General user will be able to register for the site. Design a Form which will collect users' information. Use *Spry Form validation* as far as you can. Write PHP script to process the form and *insert* the information in the MySQL database.
12. General user after registration can login the site. Create a login form for the user
13. General user can modify ONLY his/her information. Write PHP script to *update* a record
14. Admin can view all the users' information. Write PHP script to *select* the users information and display for admin user
15. ONLY admin user can *delete* member's record. Write PHP script to *delete* a record
16. Test all the functionality and show that after each operation the database remain consistent
17. In addition to the above, you are required to implement the followings:

    - Implement *hit counter* using file system
    - Implement *file upload* (test with pdf as well as image file)
    - Implement *search facility* (within document root as well as in www)
    - Use *header* function to redirect user after some operation is complete
    - Use *mailto* tag for emailing. Also experiment with PHP *mail* function

    In the final report, include the followings:

    - Write a *SQL script* that will create all the tables and populate the database

- Write a sample PHP scripts which can *select* data from database table and show the result in Web page as nice tabular fashion
- Design a sample Web Form that will match the underlying database's some table.
- Write necessary PHP scripts that will *insert* the Form's data to the underlying database table

During Summer and Fall 2011, I was working as Assistant Professor in the Department of Electrical Engineering and Computer Science (EECS), North South University (NSU). I prepared questions for MS Qualifying Exam of *Programming Language Principles* and *Database Systems*. I asked one question on *prove by induction*. Although it is very easy, some students could not answer it as in *closed form solution*. This is to say that in order to prove by induction, there are two cases: *base case* and *inductive hypothesis*. Base case can be proved just by choosing the value *n* to be some base case value like 0, 1 and show that both the left hand side (LHS) and right hand side (RHS) of the equation is the same. In case of induction, we have to prove, say the formula is true for some value *K*, then it should also be true for the value *K+1*. I remember one question was asked in my *PhD Proficiency Exam* as well in *Discrete Mathematics* to prove by induction that $\sum_{i=1}^{n} i\text{\^{}}3 = (\sum_{i=1}^{n} i)^2$. It took me a lot of time to obtain the *closed form solution*. By the way, I had to sit for PhD Proficiency Exam for four different subjects: Data Structures and Algorithms, Discrete Mathematics, Operating Systems and Object Oriented Programming. Among these, Discrete Mathematics was the hardest one. Fortunately I passed all of them in one attempt. It had been a lot of cases that PhD students can not pass one or more of the above. Later, Computer Science Department of Wayne State University omitted Operating Systems from the part of PhD Proficiency Exam.

In ACM-ICPC 2011 Dhaka Site, I was given the responsibility for sitting arrangement of hundreds of programming contest teams. To be fair, we ensured that no two teams from the same institution will sit side by side. I was supplied with the floor plan, physical arrangement of the PCs and as well the list of participants. Then I used the knowledge of *Graph Coloring* and *sampling without replacement* technique. In Computer Science Graph Coloring is a well known technique to assign color of graph so that no two adjacent nodes will have the same color. The teams' Institution names were treated as colors—two teams from same institution were NOT allocated side by side PC. Sampling without replacement is a *greedy technique*, every PCs were given some number ranging from 1..100, once a PC is allocated for a team, the same PC is not considered any more. The process should start with the highest number of teams in a institution, assign PC for all the teams of that institution considering the physical layout/position of the PCs so that no two teams are adjacent, then continue with the next highest number of teams of another institution. It worked perfectly and there was no complain. The only fix we had to do was a manual intervention: accidently two best teams from two different institutions were assigned adjacent PCs, the organizer already knew about the potentially of the teams, and they wanted them to be far apart. The whole exercise was very simple to carry out—still we had only 2-3 hours for it. So we did the whole process manually, assigning the teams in different PCs. Sometimes computer are NOT the fastest way to solve problems because writing the program would be time consuming, followed by rigorous amount of testing phase. But once the correct program has been installed, we can use it for many times *effectively* and *efficiently*. Again the input format matters and sometimes converting one input format to another takes time. This is a limitation for any computer program: the program will work only for some specified valid inputs.

I started PhD program at Wayne State University in January 2006. In the following I will discuss my experiences for the years 2006-2010.

I took a course on *Introduction to Bioinformatics*, a new emerging field in Computer Science. Bio-informatics is a discipline integrated with Computer Science, Biology, Statistics and Mathematics. I studied a lot of Bioinformatics tools, Algorithms, Databases etc. The essence of Bioinformatics problem is to search string (may be in linear time such as *Z, Boyer-Moore and Knuth-Morris-Pratt* algorithm.), computing *edit distance* between two similar gene sequence, computing *suffix tree* (also known as *trie data structure)*, find the longest common subsequence (LCS) etc. My previous knowledge from algorithms helped a lot. I studied Multiple Sequence Alignment (MSA), Protein Protein Interaction (PPI), Gene Regulatory Networks and published some research papers out of it. The entire Biological domain data can succinctly be described by 7 words: *Gene, RNA, Protein, Folding, Structure, Function and Regulation.* The expression of the genetic information stored in the DNA molecule occurs in two stages: transcription, during which DNA is transcribed into mRNA and translation, during which mRNA is translated to produce a protein DNA mRNA Protein. This is known as *central dogma of molecular biology*. The Alfinsen's Hypothesis is that protein sequences determine 3D structures, which in turn determine the function of a protein. Although Bioinformatics did not become my PhD Dissertation topic, it helped me a lot to start a solid foundation for research. Now I understand why my advisor wanted me to pursue some projects which he knew was not going anywhere. I understand I am not a Bioinformatics domain expert. I only have programming, data structures knowledge. The Biologist have their own controlled vocabulary (i.e., *ontology*), there are lot of symbols, terms etc. which is very difficult for a computer science graduate to understand. Only an active and fruitful collaboration between *computer science* and *life science* can lead to some successful end. The ultimate goal of Bioinformatics study is to develop *in silico* models that complement *in vitro* and *in vivo* biological experiments. There are three main objectives for Bioinformatics. These are:

- To develop new algorithms and statistics to access existing information in large scale databases
- To develop tools that aid in the analysis and the interpretation of those huge data
- Analyze the data in a biologically meaningful manner

I worked in a Bioinformatics project for a while. Below I am outlining the project description.

Bioinformatics Project Outline

Overview: The goal of this project is to design a program with which novel transcription factor binding sites, common to a set of genes, can be discovered. By integrating information from FlyBase, AlignACE and STAMP, a user will be able to input a set of Drosophila gene names, and obtain common binding site consensus motifs and the factors that bind them.

Method:
FlyBase: Design a program to extract sequence from a set of genes (Flybase-AlignACE). The sequence information will be extracted from www.flybase.org. The gene names and amount of sequence to be extracted *upstream* and *downstream* of the transcription start site of the genes are to be specified by the user. The amount will be the same for each of the genes entered per search. The output will thus be a defined (by the user) amount of sequence from each of the genes entered as input above.

AlignACE: Design a program to link the output from the FlyBase-AlignACE program to the AlignACE search engine (http://atlas.med.harvard.edu/cgi-bin/alignace.pl). The output from FlyBase-AlignACE will be directly entered into the AlignACE program, provided that the total amount of sequence extracted does not exceed the character limit for the AlignACE search form. At this point, the user should have the option to alter the parameters of the AlignACE search according to the AlignACE program.

After the default or other parameters have been chosen, AlignACE will search for motifs within and among the sequences entered, and will provide a series of motifs with corresponding confidence (MAP) scores. These motifs will then be entered into the STAMP search form.

STAMP: Design a program to enter output from AlignACE into the STAMP search form (www.benoslab.pitt.edu/stamp). AlignACE output consists of multiple permutations for each motif identified. At this point, a user should have the option of filtering the AlignACE output prior to entering it into the STAMP search form. AlignACE output produces 4 columns for each motif, including (1) motif sequence, (2) the particular sequence in which the motif was found, (3) the position of the site within the sequence, and (4) whether the motif is on the forward or the reverse strand of the DNA. These columns, as well as the MAP scores corresponding to each motif, can likely be used to further organize and filter the motif data. For instance, a user may wish to restrict the STAMP input to include only motifs that were identified in all of the input sequences. Likewise, a user may want to include only motifs with a particular MAP score. Such filtering options at this point will allow the user to streamline the potential data generated by the STAMP search engine. In this way, the occurrence of false positives (a factor that does not actually bind the genes in question) and negatives (failing to identify a legitimate factor or binding site) can be addressed. Lastly, the STAMP engine allows for the adjustment of various parameters including which trans factor databases to search. The user should be able to choose one or more of these databases to search. The user should also be able to adjust the other parameters (i.e., the alignment algorithm) at this point.

Additional options:

Currently, the FlyBase-AlignACE program is designed so that sequence can only be extracted based on FBgn number (FlyBase assigns an identifying number to each gene). Users will more likely enter gene names. A user may, however, wish to enter an FBgn number or CG number. Fly genes have multiple synonymous names, as well as an FBgn and a CG number associated with them. The FlyBase-AlignACE program should be modified such that a user can enter any of these, or a combination of all three, as input. Additionally, FBgn numbers are linked to their corresponding *gene ontology* (GO) annotations. Allowing users to be able to utilize this information would also be helpful. For instance, a user may know of a particular factor that binds a particular gene, and may then wish to search all of the genes sharing the ontology annotation of that gene. Linking the ontology annotations to the FBgn numbers in the FlyBase-AlignACE program will allow a user to identify binding factors by this classification also.

I did another course on *Data Analysis Techniques for Bioinformatics*. I learned the technique of statistical method for identifying *normal* and *disease* gene etc. by using techniques like t-test, p-value, e-value etc.

For the first six months of my PhD education, I studied a lot on Bioinformatics to develop some model how to integrate Protein Protein Interaction (PPI) and Gene Expression data.

I had a lot of hard time and difficulty with *Theory of Computational Complexity* course, i.e., NP-Complete problems. After reading the relevant chapter from Cormen's book of Introduction to Algorithms, my understanding become matured. I always tried to formulate any computer science problem as simple as I could. Said is another words, I always develop some *heuristics* or *rule of thumb* to relate the complex problems into one of my favorite known problem. The art of proving any problem to be NP complete is to use any known NP complete problem, then use some *polynomial time reduction* function to show that the unknown problem can be reduced to the known NP complete problem. My understanding from *Digital Logic* helped a lot to understand that given *n* input, why there can be 2^n combinations in the *truth table*. And when there is 2^n combination which is exponential, the exhaustive enumeration will fail as *n* grows. Then the only way is to check or verify the problem in polynomial time. Another type of problem needs n! permutation/ combination, those are also proved to be NP Complete. I would like to cite a sentence from Cormen book to conclude my discussion on NPC. "Class P is the class of problems which can be *solved* in polynomial time". "Class NP is the class of problems which can be *verified* in polynomial time". To understand better, we all know that to solve a problem from scratch is very hard, but if someone has already solved the problem, then to verify whether the solution is OK or not is very easy.

I enjoyed one course every semester that was graduate seminar one credit course. It was mandatory for the Graduate Teaching Assistant (GTA) to attend. For about five years of staying as PhD students, I have attended more than 100 gradate seminar talks for a wide variety of research topics. I would strongly recommend any PhD students to attend any seminar/talk held by the department for many reasons. For example, you can be linked with the researcher, can get access to the power point presentation, learn the presentation skill, have the opportunity to mingle together etc. It really helps.

Background

CSC8990 Graduate Seminar is a 1 credit course designed specially for graduate student pursuing MS or PhD in Computer Science. A MS student can take it twice, while a PhD student will be able to take it as many as 8 times. This course will bridge the gap between the academia and industry.

It will be a great help for the graduating students as they will have the opportunity to meet with different background people, discuss potential research topic, liaise with industry related personnel etc. Selected topics from computer science will be covered including software engineering, databases, distributed and parallel computing, computer vision, bioinformatics, and other topics.

Methodology

Each week student will have to meet once, Tuesday 3:00-4:20pm. Students have to write report every following week, what they have learned from past week's talk. Not only external faculty member will take part in the process, but also Wayne State University Faculty, PhD student can take part in the graduate seminar lecture series. It will create a harmonic atmosphere for the researchers to share the ideas among themselves.

Limitation

As the talk will cover a wide variety of computer science/information technology topics, we may not find it all interesting or understandable for us. Anyway, we will have to get extract as much as possible to our capacity. In the following, I will try to summarize each of the talk's abstract. Those can be found at *www.cs.wayne.edu* site.

Determinacy Inference for Logic Programs. The database of a Prolog program consists of two kinds of statements: *facts* and *rules*. Some applications of Prolog are: intelligent data base retrieval, natural language understanding, expert systems, specification language, machine learning, robot planning, graphics, problem solving. Prolog works on *depth first* and *backtracking*, the system tries to give all possible answer for the query. The main theme of the talk is how to minimize the redundant computation in logical inference.

Quality Assurance and Adaptation: A Key to Stress-Resilient Internet Services. The main idea of the talk is how to assure Quality of Service (QoS) for pervasive next generation Internet. Current Internet is termed as *Best Effort* (BE) model, that is Internet try its best to give better quality of service. The next generation of Internet has to deal with many kind of challenge. So we need a framework where the user's perceived QoS will be better. In this connection, we need the Internet to differentiate between different classes of users. The basic idea of the talk is how to create different class of users, their bandwidth requirement, delay, packet loss etc. and QoS related parameters are well taken care of. We can identify three kinds of delay associated with Web applications. These are: Network Delay, Server Delay and Browser Delay. Network delay is the time it takes for a page to travel from remote server to destination client. Server delay is the time difference when the Web server first gets the request from client and the time when it finish putting all the HTML content in the network. Browser delay is the time for a Web Browser say IE, to render the Web page contents. We see that network is not the only component which adds delay for page downloading from Internet. A lot more can be done on the server side scripting as well as modifying the Web Server kernel.

Utilizing Beam forming Antennas for Wireless Multi-hop Networks. We can identify a number of problems of wireless networks, such as *interference problem*, *signal fading* and *hidden terminal* problems. These can be partially solved using Beam Forming directional Antenna Technology.

Intelligent Coordination Design in Software Systems. We know from software engineering perspective that *cohesion and coupling* are two conflicting requirement. Now-a-days we employ the RAD^3 model (Rapid Application Design, Development and Deployment). In broader sense, software can be treated as a Service (SaaS).

Ontology-Guided Search and Text Mining for Intelligence Gathering. An ontology is a formal specification of a shared conceptualization for a domain of interest. Data Mining is the process of analyzing data to discover new patterns or relationships. Text Mining is subfield of Data Mining. We can say that text mining is the process of analyzing unstructured text to discover new patterns or relationships. In practice, Text mining often refers simply to the Content Extraction (CE) of structured data from unstructured text usually from finite-state parsers (*parsers can be bottom-up or top-down parser.*) An example of content extraction is given as follows: "Company XYZ is known to ship products through the port of Dubai". From this free text, the structured knowledge extracted as "<XYZ-Corp, exports-through, Dubai>". Here we see a triplet, a standard defined by Resource Description Framework (RDF) and Web Ontology Language (OWL).

A PhD student has to go through a tremendous amount of pressure, i.e., academic, financial, social, family-wise etc. The typical five/six years pass through straightened circumstances followed by tension to loose TA/RA ship. This is a joke that the *only way to survive in a PhD program is to procrastinate.* I had a chance to listen to a talk given by the creator of *www.phdcomics.com*, a site about the life of graduate students. The following story was told to me by some University of California Berkley graduate and I believe it is true as I had to go through the similar experiences. In a social gathering in Canton, MI, USA, he told me that there are three obstacles a PhD student has to face and successfully defending all three will eventually leads to graduation. The first attack will come during his third/fourth year in graduate studies, when his/her fund will go away. The second attack will come during fourth/fifth year from his/her advisor when they will refuse to write letter of recommendation during the job search. And the third attack will come during fifth/sixth year when she/she had got a job offer, going to convert visa status from F1 to CPT/OPT and lastly H1-B, PhD advisor will say that a lot of thing yet need to be done, you better go to continue as part time student!

The previous paragraph discussed the hardship a PhD student might go through. There are good things for PhD student as well: you have limited liability, flexible office hours etc. to take advantage of *work-life balance*. I had the opportunity to travel a lot during my two years stay as MS student at UNSW as well as during my five years stay as PhD student at Wayne State University. In the following I will try to recall my sweet memories of those.

During 1999, I was awarded AusAID scholarship to pursue MS at University of New South Wales (UNSW). The scholarship carried the return air fare between Dhaka and Sydney. First time I traveled with *Thai Airways*, we had a two hour stop over in Bangkok Airport. In an international transit, two hour break is nothing you even can't visit the *duty free shop*. From Bangkok to Sydney was about 10 hours' journey, so far the longest one in my life. We reached Sydney in due time. To me the air travel is the most boring. I was very serious in the first semester at UNSW, got *distinction* in all the courses. After finishing one semester my roommate told me that he is going for a day to *Canberra*, capital of Australia, some 300 miles away from Sydney and if I want to join him. I happily agreed and we took *Greyhound bus*. This was my first long distance highway journey in Australia. Canberra is a beautiful small city. It is renowned for Australian National University (ANU) and the Australian parliament house. We stayed the night in *Todd Hall* of ANU. In Sydney, I lived in a suburb named *Eastlake* near Sydney Airport (BTW there are about 800 suburbs in Sydney). Our favorite pastime was to visit *Circular Quay*, *Sydney Opera House* and *Harbor Bridge*. I had the opportunity to see world class spectacular *fireworks* many times in Sydney Harbor Bridge. We had a community picnic at *Blue Mountain's three sisters* some 120 miles away from Sydney. On our way back, we visited *Home bush Bay*, the home of *Sydney 2000 Olympic*. I had the chance to see live Hockey match between Canada and Malaysia in which Canada won. One day me and my room mate visited *Wollongong* some 80 mile away from Sydney by train. We spent the whole evening in the spectacular Wollongong beach. UNSW office of international students and scholar very often arranged for study tour near by Sydney, I avail three times myself of this opportunity. Once we spent a whole day in *Central Coast* which is famous for lots of *pelican birds* in a lake. Another trip was on *Hunter Valley*, famous for winery (believe me I did NOT taste any!). As a senior AusAID scholar, I had the privilege to guide new comer, I was selected to accompany 100 international AusAID scholars for *Sydney Harbor cruise*. The transport system of Sydney consisting of Bus, Train and Ferry is excellent. I can confidently say that this is unique in the world as I have seen so far. By the way, Sydney, a population of about 4 million, is one of the *top ranked 15 cities of the World*. *Bondi beach* in Sydney is a world resort for the tourist.

I knew my tenure in UNSW was going to be over soon by one more year, so I heavily traveled alone myself as far as I could. After finishing second semester, I visited Bangladesh for about a month by Singapore Airlines, transit through *Changi Airport*, by far one of the best airports of the world. I have seen there is a travel agent at UNSW campus. The students love to travel as far as they could.

I took train from Sydney to Melbourne, about 1000 Km journey for 13 hours. From Melbourne, I took another train to travel to Gippsland, stayed at my friend's home at Monash University. The next day we traveled about three hours to see *snow mountain* mount Baw Baw. In Australia, people drive five hours to see snow, in North America we have Winter season where snow last for more than four months. On my way back to Sydney by bus, I stayed in another friend's home at Melbourne downtown, visited a number of Monash University campus like Clayton, Clawfield etc. I liked traveling with tram in Melbourne city, the similar can be seen in Toronto, ON, Canada as *Street car*.

After finishing third semester, I visited *Brisbane* by air and from there to *Gold Coast* by train. I stayed in some *Backpackers* hotel, a popular and cheap rent hotel to stay. The guests spontaneously arrange Barbeque (BBQ) at night. *Surfers Paradise* is very famous resort city. I ate dinner in some Indian restaurant. The next day I had seen *Sea World* and also visited *Kurambin World Life Sanctuary*, taken photograph with *Kangaroo etc*. I had taken a lot of pictures during my tour to Brisbane (my relatives, colleagues said the pictures were the best in my appearance, used those as part of my marriage processing!)

During my last semester I applied for PhD program at University of Central Florida, USA. I got full fund to pursue PhD. Just one month before leaving Australia, I visited *Auckland, New Zealand* by China Airways for about a week. I stayed at *Backpackers* hotel in *Auckland central*. From Auckland, I visited *Rotoroa*, some 300 Km away from Auckland. It is said that Auckland is the *second largest city* by area after *Los Angeles*. Rotoroa is famous for hot spring, natural hot water emanates from underground and people can take natural hot water bath. There I watched some performance of Aboriginal people (Waikato). Also I took whole day city tour of the Auckland. I remember during the few last months, I traveled almost all the Sydney Transportation routes by Bus, Train or Ferry.

I had the first opportunity to see USA Summer in May 2006 when I accompanied some of my friends to *Cleveland*, OH. There we had seen *Lake Erie (*one of the five greatest lakes of north America, viz. Huron, Ontario, Michigan, Erie and Superior (HOMES)*)*, visited Case Western Reserve University, Cleveland State University in Downtown. I must say the Summer of USA is unparallel. The very next week we had the opportunity to visit Michigan's Upper Peninsula, some 8 hours drive from Detroit. We had cruise for about 2 hour there, seen *pictures rock*. We stayed the night somewhere near *Manisting* and *Munising*.

During end of Summer and beginning of Fall 2006, I traveled to and from Detroit to Dhaka by *Gulf Air*—transit through Bahrain, stayed at *Hotel Gulf Gate*. Although I took Sengian transit visa for Germany (Frankfurt Airport), I did not visit the city.

Although I learned driving in my home country, in Fall 2006, I took 4 lessons before driving road test in USA. I remember in the very first lesson, the instructor took me in the I-75 highway just after 5 minute of verbal briefing. I must say the speed limit which was above 60 mph was beyond any limit I had driven ever. I was very nervous, but the instructor was so good that I feel at home in quite easily. I passed the road test in one chance. It took about a week to get the driver's license. To celebrate, we rented a car from *Avis* and visited Chicago the next day. Even one of my colleagues just had Temporary Instruction Permit (TIP). Chicago is a huge city, traffic is heavy. Fortunately we had some other experienced colleague to drive at downtown Chicago. Due to lack of time, we could not visit *Sears Tower*. During Thanks Giving break, we visited Virginia and Washington DC, seen White House, visited a number of museums, seen 3D movie titled "*Walking in the Moon*". In the next day morning, although we started very early from Woodbridge, VA, we still missed to have a ride on *Washington monument*.

Fall 2006 semester was almost over. One of our friends had just defended his PhD dissertation. He joined us to a trip to *Key West, Florida*. We rented a jeep from *Enterprise*, had a week long tour traveled almost 4000 miles. We stayed at *Holiday Inn* in Key West, seen Epcot, *Disneyland in Orlando. One needs at least a full week to visit/see/ride all the items in Disneyland. We had stayed at* Sarasota, Miami, Orlando, Tampa etc. We enjoyed a day in *South beach*.

Winter 2007 was my best semester ever. I had completed almost all the required course work (got all A, A-), completed PhD qualifying Exam.

Also I had the opportunity to be an instructor for a course. Then I took a semester off from Wayne State University. I visited Bangladesh by *Kuwait Airways via* UK (London Heathrow Airport). I stayed at hotel *Safir* in Kuwait Airport. I spent the whole summer in Dhaka. I had the opportunity to teach a graduate course *Internet Engineering* in Dhaka. Just because of this experience, in one of my Skype video conferencing faculty interview some time Spring/Summer 2010, the committee members were referring to Internet Engineering, its curriculum, course content etc. In Fall2007, I took my family with me in Detroit. A new life and challenge started. In Michigan we had a lot of travel in Detroit, Ann Arbar, Canton, Troy, Madison Heights, Port Huron, Saginaw, Michigan Upper Peninsula, Kalkaska, Lansing), OH (Toledo, Columbus) etc.

One day I traveled to Saginaw to attend a birthday party. On our way back home in Detroit, the *timing belt* of my car was broken near Flint, MI, some 70 mile away from Detroit. I had to tow the car back to Detroit. As I had only basic coverage from Automobile Association of America (AAA), I had to pay about $280 and the car repair cost was about $250. This is a joke that I tell my friends, what can be a cost to attend a birthday party!

In 2008, one of my research papers got accepted in some conference held at Los Angeles. We traveled by Spirit airways to LA. We visited *Malibu beach, Beverly Hills, Santa Monica beach, Hollywood boulevard, Universal Studio.* Later I had the chance to visit *Bakersfield,* some 115 away from LA. One day we visited San Diego via highway 5, seen *La Jolla* beach. California has the longest scenic drive in USA. The combination of mountain and the Pacific Ocean made it unique in the world. One of our friends' commented "*God has created California, 1100 miles driving belt in His own hand*".

I had the chance to visit Chicago, IL 4 times. Lake Shore Drive was a pleasant experience. Seeing 5 states from top of *Sears Tower* was a memorable event. I can't forget the *Devon* area because of Asian cultural ethnicity. We stayed near *Palatine.* We had the chance to visit nearby Lake Front Park, Glencoe Beach, Round Lake Beach, Grays Lake, Antioch, Gurnee Mills etc. One day my friend drove me near Wisconsin (Kansasville). Two times I traveled to Chicago by *Greyhound Bus,* we had stop over at Kalamazoo, Jackson and Gary (Indiana).

In August 2008, one of our relatives from London, UK visited us in Detroit. He has visited USA many a times, but never seen *Niagara Fall,* which is about 4 hours drive from Detroit. So we decided to treat him for the first time in Niagara Fall. As we already become Canadian Permanent Resident, it was easy for us to drive through *Windsor* to Niagara Fall. We came back the same day.

From end of 2008 and beginning of 2009, we started living in Windsor, Canada. I used to commute to and from Windsor and Detroit 3-4 times a week. Crossing USA-Canada border so many times via Detroit-Windsor Tunnel or Ambassador Bridge was unique experiences for me. I think I can write another book solely on my experience to cross USA-Canada border.

I have traveled almost all the nearby Windsor cities/towns: Leamington, Pelee Island National Park, Amhurstburg, LaSalle, Wheatley Bay, Kingsville, Tilbury, Chatham, Kent, Blenheim, Sarnia, Ridge Town (Green View Aviaries). Berry picking during summer was a lot of fun.

I have traveled Toronto, the financial hub of Canada 4 times. We visited Scarborough town center, Danforth, Gerard etc. London is 187 Km away from Windsor. One day we visited University of Western Ontario in London, ON a beautiful campus.

In August 2009, we had visited North Carolina (Raleigh, Winston-Salem, Charlotte, Durham), Georgia (Atlanta). I would recommend visiting *Stone Mountain* in Atlanta. We also visited Virginia, Washington DC, seen *white house*. In 5 days, I alone drove more that 2500 miles.

In November 2009, I visited Hong Kong to present a research paper. After 4 hours of fly over Atlantic Ocean, the pilot of the airplane announced that he has not observed in the last 22 years of his career, they are experiencing some technical difficulty (*hydraulic failure*) so instead of going to Japan, coming back to Washington. Anyway, it was a normal landing. We were given hotel and meal voucher. So I had the opportunity to stop over *Seattle Tacoma* Airport and stayed a night at *Coast Gateway* Hotel. Also Delta airlines provided us flight coupon worth $200, which I *redeemed* within a year. In Hong Kong I stayed at *Marriott Hotel*. In Hong Kong, I had seen City Central, ifc Mall, Peak, Kowloon, Tsing Yi, Asia World-Expo. Among these, *Peak* is the most attractive to visit. I posted over 100 photo of Hong Kong visit in my *face book*. I must say the language the Hong Kong people use is horrible to understand. On my way back transit was through Japan (Tokyo Narita International Airport). I also had more than 6 hours of stop over in Minnesota Minneapolis Airport. Therefore I use tram to see the *twin city*.

In 2010, we visited Ottawa, Montreal and Quebec City. I alone drove more than 2000 Km. In Ottawa, we had seen a city called *Kanata*, actually the country name Canada is originated from Kanata which means village. We had seen Dawes Park, Midway Family Fun Park, Science & Technology Museum in Ottawa. In Montreal we visited downtown, Old Port, Olympic Park and of course Concordia University. Quebec City, the capital of Quebec is about 250 Km away from Montreal. The scenic beauty of Quebec city is beyond description.

In 2010-2011 I had traveled extensively in the Mountain Zone, USA: Montana (Billings, Red Lodge, Yellow stone National Park), Colorado (Denver), Utah (Salt Lake City Airport), Wyoming (Sheridan), North Dakota (Baker).

In 2011 I had traveled Bangladesh two times by Emirates Airlines, transit through UAE (Dubai Airport). I had transit through Texas (Houston George W. Bush International Airport) and Arizona (Phoenix Airport).

Two things I will recommend any PhD students to master: *Latex* and *Power Point Presentation*. Although, now-a-days, Microsoft Word has advanced options to compose graphics, equation etc., I think Latex will dominate the research and publications world for long time because of its ease of composing as text and enriched set of *mark ups*. I remember that I did NOT know latex till my PhD Qualifying Exam when my advisor said he will NOT accept any writing composed other than latex. It took me only a week to produce some pdf document from Latex still it gave me a hard time to *embed* graphics due to configuration problems as encapsulated postscript file (eps). Later I used to use graphics package for Portable Network Graphics (png) file. Now-a-days, almost all the conferences (e.g., ACM/IEEE) and journal provide template for latex document and you just start composing. Said in my advisor's word "*Nothing can be easier than Latex*". For the presentation skill, I would recommend any one as *one third rule*: one third of the presentation is for all the *general audiences*, one third is for the *domain experts* and the rest one third is *only for you* to understand. Another tips regarding presentation: *one slide one minute*. During my graduate seminar presentation at Wayne State University for about one hour, I had prepared 96 slides, I had to skip some and pass over very quickly. Then I learned that one slide for a minute is the best. Another tip: *never ever write anything which you don't understand and can't explain*.

Let me write some tips on how to conduct research and publish paper. A PhD student need to *read more, write more and think abstractly*. Research is very time consuming, it takes time to get into research. The very first paper on a research topic might take about 2/3 years of work. But once a student can publish something new, another ten papers can be published very quickly. A PhD student may need to read hundreds of papers, not all of them are of interest to him/her. *Reading hard copy print out is at least 6 times faster than reading on screen*. So I would recommend, *skim first, if it is of interest, print*. It is said that a PhD student should start the research on the very first day of PhD program and everyday learn something new and add it to the dissertation. That is, everyday incremental progress is a key to long term success. Choosing research topic is another challenge. It is said that if you can *define* the problem, you can *solve* it. All the famous innovation's basic is very simple to understand, but the credit goes to who invented the idea first. Brainstorming with advisor helps a lot, although most of the time students are frustrated on the discussion outcome. I remember I had to make presentation every other week. Reading someone else's research paper (may be it was his/her 2/3 years of research work) and understand to give presentation in front of 10/12 PhD students is not a matter of joke. Computer Science is all about notation. Students need to understand the notation and follow the symbolic meaning of those, then try to relate them in real life applications. The same principle I heard from a Computer Science Professor regarding how to use *lambda reduce/lambda calculus*. Programming in any Artificial Intelligence (AI) language like Prolog might be useful to understand the meaning of *free* and *bound* variable which are related to the concept of *lambda reduce*.

This paragraph is intended to shed some light on the PhD advisor selection. By default, any PhD student is assigned an advisor during the first year. Students have the right to change it later. I will recommend if student-advisor relationship do not match, then change advisor only by the end of first year. It happened that some student changed advisor after three years, and it is taking another four years to complete his degree! PhD advisor don't want to publish research papers in lower tier conferences/ journal and at the same time student want to get rid of the publication barrier by trying to publish in easy going venue where *probability of acceptance* is higher. Students somehow need to balance the approach tactfully and not to hurt the advisor. It is said that time is the best healer, as time passes by, the relationship between student and advisor become deeper. I can cite one example from me. My advisor once wanted to ask me some question, but he didn't, as he already knew what might be my answer! It has been a lot of cases that students get frustrated by the outcome of brainstorming and argument with advisor. It is said that "if you can't beat your advisor then just enjoy what he says". During the first two years, active research may not be pursued due to graduate course work pressure. It is better to try to publish anything as part of the course requirement. It is also helpful if fruitful collaboration can be made with peer students and other research groups. It will help to increase the number of papers published. It is said that *quality* matters, but sometimes *quantity* matters as well. Professional membership like ACM/IEEE might help to get reduced price for conference registration. Students should try to look around local venues for publication as it might save travel/accommodation cost of attending conferences. I would suggest PhD students to do anything which you can write in your CV. As for example, our advisor was assigned to review a lot of papers, as he had limited time, we had the chance to do the initial review of the papers. Some of my referees, a conference chair, created user name and password for me to download and review some papers. I reviewed one which seems close to my research area and refused to review some other which was not in my research area. There are some graduate level courses offered as seminar course. The instructor in charge delivers some preliminary topics as first two/three weeks, then students have to present in turn for the rest of the semesters. I remember I was invited to give presentation based on my already published research papers. The presentation opportunity might be available in nearby Universities as well. Graduate students should try to attend professional talks/seminar/conferences and should build there own professional network. Now-a-days, *www.linkedin.com* is a very popular site for this purpose. I remember one of my colleague send me the invitation to join LinkedIn, then within two years my connections exceeded 500+. You never know who you will need in your life, so never ever burn any bridge.

There are some *plans of work* for PhD program, designated credit hours and courses to be taken. In addition to this, it might be beneficial to *observe* some courses informally. I remember I was a *grader* for a graduate level course. I had time, so I used to sit in the class with the students, talk to them and make friendly relation with the students. It is said that teachers not only teach, but also they learn from students. A lot of understanding can be made just by asking questions. I always asked my students to ask me question so that I can refresh my knowledge about the topic.

Take advantage of the social gathering. It is said that professional never eat only lunch, they do the business at the same time.

PhD is the art of making the ability to *reduce* a 20 pages document into one page and also make you able to *enhance* a one page document into 20 pages. This is something a PhD student must learn how to do the vice versa. A PhD Dissertation must be focused on one fundamental contribution. Carefully read a lot of related research papers and accumulate from others what fits your need. It is said that what you are looking for will NOT be found in one paper, you have a read a lot, hundreds may be thousands. I remember I was presenting a paper in some software engineering and data engineering conference. I added too many topics in the discussion. One of the audiences, some CS professor told me not to fool the PhD Dissertation committee with too many things, just concentrate about only one of the slides and that will be enough for a PhD topic. Actually she was referring to one of my related research: *given informal user requirement analysis how to automatically build the concept hierarchy or populate the ontology*.

I was fortunate to attend almost all the conferences where my papers were accepted. In case of journal paper, there is no need to make presentation. In conferences/workshop/symposium etc. at least one author should register and attend/present the paper. This is some ethical issue that Computer Science professional should follow otherwise the charm of conferences will fade away soon.

This is a tip that I want to share with any PhD students: whatever idea comes in your mind, please write it down otherwise you might forget it soon. I heard from one Computer Science professor that it took only *five minute* to solve his PhD problem. I remember it took me about *two hours* to code the main algorithm of my dissertation. Please note that five minute or two hours, these are time referring to the final and last stage of the problem, it take a long time to define and formulate the problem, its dimension, exceptions, pre processing, post processing etc. When I shared my PhD research idea/ topic with my fellow group, everybody appreciated and some one told me that he will do it for me in three days! Again, said in my advisor's word, "great idea is something which is very easy to understand".

Another tip for PhD students: whenever you want to present something, prepare one small *running example* that you will refer to time and again in the talk.

I had a lot of hard time making any progress in my PhD Dissertation research. Sometimes I get frustrated. I told my inability to progress to one of my PhD dissertation committee member, he said, "*it is good that you are nervous*". Actually the professor had so far graduated more than 25 PhDs, he knows what a PhD student might go through. Another difficulty I faced for NOT to find relevant/related research papers. My advisor said, "*it is even better*". That means as my research topic is very new it will open up new opportunities. There was an embarrassing situation for me. One day, I was doing programming experiment with Google. I was sure that my program is OK, so I called my advisor to see the result in the lab. He came down stair to see the experiment. To my utter surprise, the program was NOT running anymore! I was very upset. I thought my advisor will mean otherwise that I might have given him bluff. But he assured me that sometimes thing might go wrong. Although assured by my advisor, I was tenacious to dig into the matter. And I found that Google was blocking *automated user query*. I took the *screen shot* of what Google was reporting and showed those to my advisor. Later, I had to use Yahoo! Build Your Own Search Service (BOSS) API to carry out my experiments which allows unlimited automated query a day.

I had worked as Graduate Teaching Assistant (GTA) and Instructor during 2006-2010. Below I try to recall some of the events I faced as GTA or instructor. I started GTA job with C programming during the very first semester. One notorious thing of C language I wish to share with everyone: the same symbol * is used for *multiplication* and *pointer dereferencing*. My expectations from the students were very high, whereas students came from a diverse population and background. Although I was very sincere in taking the lab, at the end of semester, my evaluation was not that good. Later I learned how to keep pace with the students demand. In Spring/Summer 2006, I had been appointed as Instructor for discrete mathematics course. One of the students was very much struggling to grasp the course material. He used to visit me in my office hours. I asked what grade he is expecting of the course. He said B. At the end of the semester, he got B+. I use this example thorough out my teaching career: I say to the students at the beginning of the semester not to worry about the grade, just to concentrate learning something from the course and your grade will be at least one point higher than your expectation. One of the faculties had negative attitude towards me or on my capability. So I wanted to be his TA. Ultimately in one semester I was his TA, worked hard for the course. At the end of the semester, he evaluated me as outstanding and commented "I was very impressed with Emdad's work ethic and quality of work this semester. I was very happy that he was the grader for this course." By the way, I had been GTA for about 10 semesters. Below I am copying all the comments (if any) made by faculty on my Graduate Teaching Assistant Evaluation form:

- Very professional—outstanding work
- Very professional, required zero supervision. Would be happy to work with again
- Emdad has been a completely dependable, hard working and skilled TA. I will miss his effort and dedication the first time that I have to teach 6580 without him
- Emdad is a great TA. He is very punctual and in general has a good grasp of the subject matter
- Emdad was very responsive to my requests and performed his tasks (e.g., grading, solution writing) quickly and effectively
- Outstanding

During 2009-2010 I had to learn Python as part of being lab instructor for introductory programming course. As I did not use Python before, I was reluctant to be GTA for the course. Then the department chair said "Are you afraid to learn a new programming language?" My answer was NO. Then I served as GTA for about a year. The morale of the story is: you always have to be prepared to face something new every time.

I would suggest PhD students to submit research paper whenever it is possible, even if you know that the probability of acceptance is below 15%. By submitting paper in high ranked/tier conferences, you will get experts review/feedback free of cost. I must confess that *my papers were rejected a number of times*. But every time I got feedback from the reviewers, I tried my best to address the concerns raised by them. It helped me a lot to improve my paper. Actually experts give opinion at a very high level with little amount of textual description. I am now discussing 29 such questions that I had to address in my PhD Dissertation although I had submitted this at least 5-6 times to the PhD Dissertation committee, graduate school etc. In the answer, I am mentioning the page number of my PhD Dissertation where the relevant discussions have been made.

1. **Concern:** It is NOT intuitive that user will issue queries in SQL-way
   Answer: Our work in motivated by Google Base beta version for structured query over Web Data. (Pg 3)
2. **Concern:** The process is NOT fully automated
   Answer: Since wrappers are built automatically, the values that they extract are anonymous and a human intervention is still required to associate a meaningful name to each data item. Our novel research problem is: given wrapper generated tables and a candidate set of labels, the label assignment is fully automatic. Human intervention is ONLY required to choose from a ranked list of labels for the final annotation (Pg 3)
3. **Concern:** What are the drawbacks of work already done in this field and how you have overcome the limitations?
   Answer: Previous approaches to labeling have two drawbacks. (Pg 4)
4. **Concern:** Will the approach be scalable towards Web data integration?
   Answer: We have implemented a number of prototype systems. Our approach to labeling will supplement these systems. (Pg 5)
5. **Concern:** What is the research issue?
   Answer: Given a candidate set of labels and anonymous datasets, can Web search engines such as Google, Yahoo and MSN be used to assign labels for the anonymous datasets? There is certainly potential for the research direction explored by this paper, i.e., the automatic assignment of meaningful labels to anonymous database tables. Wide-scale Web mining over deep Web databases will require this. (Pg 6)
6. **Concern:** What is the research contribution?
   Answer: We propose specific method, Web search engine based annotator, to solve the problem without the support of domain ontology. In our method, domain ontologies are not required any more. Specifically we bridge the gap between two orthogonal research viz., *wrapper generation* and *label extraction* for value added services such as online comparison shopping. It is worthy. It is interesting and novel to use this for the task of labeling anonymous database tables. (Pg 8)
7. **Concern:** The function omega seems to be never introduced in the paper
   Answer: We just defined it and work on the post processing part of it. (Pg 9)
8. **Concern:** A bigger drawback of the paper is that mature commercial systems such as *Google Squared* which solve the same problem were left out of the comparison

Answer: Google Squared solved the problem this way: Given a concept, find instances of the concept. We address the problem differently. Our approach is: Given instances and a candidate set of labels, assign which labels correspond to the instances. (Pg 20-23)

9. **Concern:** Does the predefined label correspond to the term used in the database schema or to the term in the user query. How is the matching done?
   Answer: For Web data integration, there is no pre-defined database schema. We will construct the schema on-the-fly and try to satisfy user query. There is no schema matching involved. (Pg 23)
10. **Concern:** Although you give references for BAMM and RoadRunner, the paper is not self-contained enough in giving the reader a hint what those datasets are.
    Answer: BAMM datasets @ UIUC worked on how to extract Web form labels from hidden Web sources. RoadRunner datasets produced wrapper generated tables without labels. We bridge the gap between these two orthogonal research by our proposed method of labeling. (Pg 23)
11. **Concern:** It is hard to find candidate labels?
    Answer: This is a challenging problem. Therefore we limit our interest to a specific domain like book, automobile, movie, music etc. and work with a limited candidate set of labels. (Pg 23)
12. **Concern:** Do you assume L to be the most general, or specific concept?
    Answer: We assume those to be the most general. (Pg 23-25)
13. **Concern:** Actually, you may find L subsumed by L_1, subsumed by L_2. Then, which L_i are you considering as the most appropriate and why?
    Answer: We assume that the candidate set of labels are flattened, in our case there is no hierarchy in concept label (Pg 23-25)
14. **Concern:** How is your approach in case you do not assume a single element a column?
    Answer: There is no difference of labeling method whether it is a column of values or a single element. Our algorithm LADS is equally applicable (Pg 28)
15. **Concern:** In terms of performance, is it reasonable to refer to a search engine with each possible pair?
    Answer: Our algorithm LADS refer to search engine as "all L and a random subset of V". (Pg 28)
16. **Concern:** You state that there are labels that do not appear in any query interface or query results and that this is exactly the difficulty that you address with your work. My question: why do you want

to label attributes that are not used, and hence do not need to be identified?
Answer: This is because of local interface schema inadequacy problem. (Pg 28-30)

17. **Concern:** What is the sub-index s in the definition of the final candidate set of labels?
    Answer: s refer to labels that will be found in SELECT clause of user query (Pg 31)
18. **Concern:** Are only 3 patterns used?
    Answer: There are around 10. We used 5 of them to plot the experimental results. (Pg 39-43)
19. **Concern:** What is PMI-IR?
    Answer: Point-wise Mutual Information for Information Retrieval. We re-defined it to be PMI(L, V) in our labeling context. (Pg 43-44)
20. **Concern:** Why your approach is better?
    Answer: Shown in section 3.8 Complexity Analysis of LADS (Pg 48-49)
21. **Concern:** How do you define favorable?
    Answer: By number of *matches* and *mismatches* (Pg 50)
22. **Concern:** The mismatches on labeling will eventually increase as the data size gets larger—will it scale?
    Answer: We assume homogeneous datasets. Data size is NOT a problem. (Pg 52-54)
23. **Concern:** Evaluations are somewhat anecdotal rather than on reliable benchmarks
    Answer: Information Extraction (IE) benchmarks in this area are not well developed. (Pg 56-60)
24. **Concern:** You need to convince the committee with large datasets
    Answer: Done, included a section Experiment with Large Datasets (Pg 61-62)
25. **Concern:** The experiments are based on small scale datasets
    Answer: Information Extraction (IE) benchmarks in this area are not well developed. Included a section 4.4 Experiment with Large Datasets (Pg 61-63)
26. **Concern:** When we talk about DSC violation, we do not mean injecting a couple of overlapping values in one column and see if hit or miss that value and how correctly the column annotation was done
    Answer: Included a section solely on impact of DSC violation (Pg 63-64)
27. **Concern:** What will happen in case DSC assumption does NOT hold?
    Answer: Included a section 4.5 Non-ideal Datasets and Impact of DSC Violation (Pg 63-65)

28. **Concern:** You cannot experiment with large dataset because Google would block you. Did you find out how to bypass that? Such as requesting for an override from Google, Yahoo and so on?
    Answer: Firstly we experimented with Google. Then when we noticed that Google is blocking automated query (more than 1000 query per day), we experimented with Google AJAX search API. Still that could not solve the problem. Then we experimented with Yahoo! (it allowed 5000 query per day). Very recently Yahoo! has released their BOSS (Build your Own Search Service) API, it allow unlimited query per day. We included a section in the dissertation based on results from Yahoo! BOSS API on large scale datasets. (Pg 66)
29. **Concern:** This paper discusses NUM, RPS, and DSC. Can every column be categorized as one of these three types?
    Answer: Our algorithm LadsComplete put an order on labeling: NUM first, followed by RPS, followed by DSC. (Pg 67)

Those were the concerned raised by reviewers and I tried my best to answer the same. The anonymous reviewers had a lot of good remarks about my work as well. I am mentioning some of them as follows:

- It is possible to transform a structured set of data obtained from a Website, e.g., the results of a query in a movie Website, into a table. Given such a table, this paper addresses the problem of assigning labels to each of its column. The set of labels is known in advance, e.g., by consulting the labels of the fields of the form in which the query was entered. The goal is then to assign each label to the correct column. The approach used by the authors consists in entering search queries of the form "label-column value" into popular search engines such as Google, and to use the number of reported hits to compute the probability that a given label is correct for a given column.
- In this paper, the authors present a method for assigning labels to unstructured datasets gleaned from Websites. The data is assumed to have been formatted into tables by an information extraction system and the goal is to assign labels to the columns such that the label assigned corresponds to the values contained in that column. This is accomplished by submitting (label, value) pairs to a number of search engines and using the hit counts returned by the search engines as a measure of correlation for each pair.
- The ideas behind the authors' method of using search engine results to assign labels to unstructured Web data seem plausible and promising.

- The paper targets an important problem of labeling anonymous datasets.
  The figures and tables have been very helpful in understanding the paper. The paper is of good cross disciplinary value. It can be helpful in machine learning techniques, biological studies, etc., to categorize anonymous datasets.
- This is an interesting paper on automatic labeling techniques for structured data utilizing Web search engines.
- The idea of the paper is good and worthy the dedication.
- The main craftsmanship of the paper is they inference the relationship of two strings by checking the statistics of their pair wise appearance on the Web with the help of a search engine.
- This method is useful when the column names of the results are not available.
- The idea is interesting and the experimental results are encouraging.
- The paper is well presented, balancing theoretical work and experimentation.
- The work presented in this paper is interesting and seems to fit very well the goals of the conference.

During last year of any PhD program is very crucial. There is a time limit set by the department that a PhD student will NOT be funded for more than 5/6 years. Therefore it is important that PhD student learn necessary skills to prepare them for the job market. Students must know their *strengths and weaknesses* and apply in different R&D/industry/faulty job accordingly. Internship is a great way to be connected in job. I had an opportunity to do internship for a semester at Montana State University Billings. In the following, I am copying the report that I submitted at the end of the internship.

Computer Science Internship

Curricular Practical Training (CPT) Report

Executive Summary

Curricular Practical Training (CPT) is an integral part of academic program. During the last year of graduate academic program, student is expected to learn hands on practical real life problem that they want to take as career. CSC6995 is a one credit course (grade S or U only) to meet this goal. Specifically student get job offer letter from employer, academic advisor approves the course and then Office of International Student and Scholar (OISS) advisor process the legal document paper works, i.e., endorse I-20 with CPT recommendation.

This report contains all the lessons learned from valuable academic experience from Montana State University Billings (MSU-B), College of Technology. MSU-B is mainly an undergraduate school, with a few exceptions of graduate level courses in Business (MBA etc.).

After a rigorous selection process, I was offered an Instructor position at MSU-B. I was assigned to conduct 16 credit courses comprise of 4 different subjects: Visual Basic, Advanced Visual Basic, Java and Advanced Web Programming. In the report I will try to enumerate all the experiences I gained here in the last 3 months at MSU-B.

This report also contains guideline how to pursue career in teaching. I hope this will be a valuable source of reference for the students who wish to take this challenging path.

1. Introduction and Background

I joined Computer Science PhD program at Wayne State University, Detroit, USA during January 2006. I passed PhD proficiency Exam in Winter2006. During that time there was 4 core courses in the PhD proficiency Exam: Data Structures; Discrete Mathematics; Operating Systems and Object Oriented Programming using C++. Fortunately I passed all the courses in first attempt. It had been a lot of cases that students could not pass one or more subjects, later Computer Science department dropped Operating Systems from the PhD proficiency Exam. I passed PhD Qualifying Exam during Winter2007, PhD Prospectus Exam on Winter2009. At the same time I completed all the required course work and dissertation credits. I made up my mind to look for faculty position. From then on, I applied more than 200 applications and continuously tried for the last 18 month to find a position. The competition was high. It had been the cases there were as low as 40 candidates for a position and as high as 400. Fortunately, I was offered Instructor position at Montana State University Billings from Fall2010.

2. Academic Job Search Check List

In the following, I am enumerating all the steps, documents etc., one need to pursue academic career. All these I learned from my own experiences from last 18 months.

1. Prepare a CV for *research University*, highlighting your expertise.
2. Prepare another CV for *teaching University* (may be 4-year college), highlighting your programming and database skill
3. Prepare another CV for *Industry* (mentioning all the tools and technique that you can sale, e.g., *algorithmic* and *coding skill*)
4. Search job in the following sites for academic positions:
    a. Higher Ed jobs
    b. Chronicle of Higher education
    c. Academic keys
    d. www.cra.org
    e. ACM Communication magazine
    f. IEEE job site
5. Every time you apply for a job, be responsive, meaning what the employer want, mention those in the cover letter and say that you are confident about those

6. You need to mention at least 3-4 persons who will write letter of recommendations for you
7. Need a teaching statement document (3-4 pages).
8. Need a research statement document (3-4 pages).
9. Need all your past students' teaching evaluation
10. Need to mention some recent sample publications
11. Need a copy of Official/Unofficial academic transcript
12. Need sample course handout for the courses you conducted

3. Interview Process

Applying online in different Web sites is only half of the game. Employers ONLY contact short listed candidate. Therefore sometimes it is very frustrating NOT to get any call. In the year 2009 the situation was very bad. Fortunately as economy was recovering, I got a number of responses from different universities beginning Spring 2010. Email acknowledgement of the application was available for most of the cases. The next step was telephone interview. For some academic institutions, they offered Video conferencing as well. I avail one of them using *Skype*. During Fall2010, I get about five calls from different academic institutions. Some of those did not proceed further due to legal document paper works (e.g., student with only F-1 visa are NOT eligible for full time work in USA and at the same time OISS will NOT issue I-20 endorsed with CPT/OPT unless there is some solid offer letter from employer—this is a vicious cycle). After successful telephone interview, I was offered on site interview from MSU-B. They covered the whole expenses (i.e., air fare, hotels etc.). I must admit their hospitality.

The interview process was very rigorous: firstly meeting with dean, meeting with a panel of 5 faculty members, mock class room presentation etc. MSU-B offer about 25 courses related to my area of expertise. The first question was asked: which of the courses among the list I am NOT ready to teach? Given sufficient time in advance, I can teach any courses in Computer Science. Anyway, I mentioned some of the certificate courses (e.g., SCJP, OCP, MCSE etc.) vendor certification courses which I did NOT do myself). The panel asked a lot of questions, I can't remember all of them, mostly *psychological questions*. One question was: tell me a situation where you make some unpleasant decision about student and how did you handle this? I answered one example from my own experience: I used to use grading curve, i.e., letter grade is assigned based on point out of 100. But the scale is not fixed. It depends on the overall class performance. We need to put a cutting point for two successive grades. In the process, some of the student may lose the higher grade, may be just for the lack of a point. I give careful consideration to make a cutting point. Still some student may be victim, but I never compromised whatever scheme I come up with. That was my answer and the penal was very pleased to know my answer.

4. About MSU-B

Montana State University Billings has been an integral part of the Billings community and a student-centered learning environment since its early days as Eastern Montana College. Founded in 1927, the University continues to nurture a longstanding tradition of educational access, teaching excellence, civic engagement and community enhancement in an urban setting. In the classroom and in the community, students receive a well-rounded unique education and training for Associate's, Bachelor's and Master's degrees for careers through the University's six colleges—arts and sciences, business, allied health professions, education, technology and professional studies and lifelong learning.

Set in the largest city in the state, Montana State University Billings and the community of *Billings* combine for a unique college experience: engaged and encouraging faculty; friendly people; a supportive community; and incredible educational opportunities. Residents of Billings have a long track record of supporting the university through scholarships, internships and civic engagement. A regional retail, financial and medical hub, Billings offers vast array of job opportunities, personal connections and leadership opportunities via three campuses spread through the city.

Life on the main campus mirrors that of Billings: Students are happy to mingle on some of the 110 park-like acres at the base of the spectacular Rimrocks or take part in a variety of cultural, service, athletic or educational activities. Whether a motivated honors student or first-generation attendee, all learners will find challenges that fulfill both individual goals and societal needs. Montana State University Billings offers pre-professional and certification programs and awards degrees at the associate's, Bachelor's and master's degree levels. MSU Billings also offers post-master's (non degree) supervisor endorsement programs. Academic Accreditation: Montana State University Billings is accredited by the Northwest Commission on Colleges and Universities. It is accredited by the National Council for the Accreditation of Teacher Education for preparing elementary and secondary teachers and school counselors through the Bachelor of Science and Master of Education degrees and the Master of Science in Special Education degree. MSU Billings is also accredited by:

- Association to Advance Collegiate Schools of Business
- Commission on Accreditation of Athletic Training Education
- National Association of Schools of Music
- National Association of Schools of Art and Design
- Council on Rehabilitation Education

5. Details of the courses

I conducted 4 courses here in MSU-B: Java; Visual Basic; Advanced Visual Basic and Advanced Web Programming. For Java, we used *Eclipse platform* and the text book was Java How to Program, by Paul Deitel and Harvey Deitel, 8th edition 2010. For Visual Basic, we used Visual Studio 2005/2008/2010. Students used 2005/2008, I myself used *Visual Studio 2010*. The text books were: Microsoft Visual Basic 2008 Reloaded by Diane Zak, 3rd edition 2010 and Microsoft Visual Basic 2005 Reloaded: Advanced by Richard A. Johnson and Diane Zak. For Advanced Web Programming, we used *Dreamweaver CS4* and *XAMPP* environment. The text book was: Dreamweaver CS4 The Missing Manual by David Sawyer McFarland. The class sizes range from 8 to 18. One problem I encountered: there is no teaching assistant or grader. All the quizzes, mid term exam, project etc., I had to grade by myself. Therefore I resort to a limited number of tests, say not more than 3-4 for the whole semester. In addition to taking classes all day long, I used to hold regular office hours. I hardly had any leisure time other than weekend.

6. Conclusions

It has been an excellent opportunity for me to work full time as faculty at MSU-B. This is just the beginning. I am looking forward to University teaching and research tenure track position. The experiences that I gained here will certainly help me to further endeavor the process. I know this will NOT be an easy job. But I hope for the best.

PhD students sometimes need to write *proposal for research funding*. Below I am outlining one such example of mine.

Description of Project Goals and Objectives

Most of the existing Web data extraction systems cannot assign field labels to the extracted data records. Most of the systems are heuristic based and can solve the labeling problem partially. Here in our research, we wish to develop a complete framework for data labeling, holistic column name assignment. We are working on the post processing part of Web wrapper and show that our labeling process yields better results on structured data such as wrapper generated Web page table. There is a high demand for collecting data of interest from multiple Web databases. For example, a comparison-shopping system (e.g., shopping.com, pricegrabber.com) needs to collect the price, availability, and other information of the same product from multiple providers. Such kinds of applications require that the collected data be semantically labeled so that they can be appropriately organized/stored for subsequent analysis.

This research proposes a method to automatically assign column names to wrapper generated tables. The work intends to develop a framework to automatically label unstructured data from extracted Web data. This method is useful when the column names of the results are not available. The input to this method includes a set of labels (extracted from Web form or query) and the result table values. The novel idea is to use Web search engines such as Google as an external knowledge base. Queries are issued over the label and values such that the pair with the highest probability (computed through *hit counts* or Label Attribute Affinity (LAA)) will be selected.

A large number of wrappers generate tables without column names for human consumption because the meaning of the columns are apparent from the context and easy for humans to understand, but in emerging applications, labels are needed for autonomous assignment and schema mapping where machine try to understand the tables. Autonomous label assignment is critical in volume data processing where ad hoc mediation, extraction and querying are involved. We are envisioning another layer of Web data abstraction where user can query intra Web document table like structure.

Our research focuses on issues related to Web information retrieval and Web information integration. In particular, we are focusing on categorizing and classifying data collections into meaningful groups. This direction of research is essential in the field of autonomous information integration and data aggregation where autonomous systems collect information from Internet resources having no proper labels. In such situations, query systems fail to identify required information and cause the production of wrong responses. Our focus in this research is on generating useful labels for groups of data items to facilitate successful query computation. We need to develop a framework which is able to query search Web forms and the Web page tables in a SQL-like way.

Given wrapper generated anonymous datasets and a candidate set of labels, can Web search engines such as Google, Yahoo, MSN be used to assign label for the anonymous datasets? Our research supports this research hypothesis. The principle idea behind our method is using a Web search engine as a knowledge base. The main craftsmanship of the research is we infer the relationship of two strings by checking the statistics of their pair wise appearance on the Web with the help of a search engine. In our approach we use "every L and a random subset of V". We have used method based on term co-occurrence to find the relation between labels and values. It is built on the basis of a fundamental hypothesis: if two terms often co-occur in the same window unit then they are considered to be *semantically* associated.

We have shown our approach based on small scale datasets and found the results to be favorable. Our data size wasn't that large in evaluation. In order to do experiments in large scale, one need special permission from search engine like Google. Otherwise Google may block the automated user query. That is one of the reasons why our results are based on small scale datasets. Information Extraction (IE) benchmarks in this area are not well developed. We have used BAMM datasets from UIUC Web data integration repositories as well as from RoadRunner Datasets. BAMM datasets contains "query schemas" each of which is a set of query attributes, extracted from Web query interfaces in 4 domains: Books, Automobiles, Movies and Music Records. Each domain consists of about 50 sources. In RoadRunner, extracted data fields are specified with labels {A, B, C, . . .}. We have shown an approach, Web Search Engine Based Annotator, to holistically assign column labels based on small scale datasets.

This research considers automatic labeling techniques for structured data generated by wrappers over hidden Web sources. The annotation problem is certainly interesting and can greatly improve the usability of automatically-generated wrappers. We have presented our work balancing theoretical work and experimentation. We have proposed that candidate set of labels will come from two sources: Web form label and user query variables. In spite of having a tag in the HTML specification called label for the declaration of a label, it is almost not used and, therefore, there isn't any explicit mechanism identifying which label is related to each field. Given the wide variation in Web form layout, even within a well-defined domain, automatically extracting Web form labels is a challenging problem. Collecting user query variables is straightforward from SELECT clause in SQL query. The approach has its use in data integration where tables are generated by a wrapper and we need to map the output variables to the columns so that we can pick the ones PROBABLY intended by the user. Traditionally user has to navigate each Web site manually. If a Web data integration system as envisioned by ours is present, user has to submit the query once and system will do the rest on-the-fly. The planned use of our approach is especially for the automated agents which try to *link* and *combine* data from different Web sources having no proper labels.

I have preliminary results for the above research. We wish to publish those in the dynamic Web site. Information Extraction (IE) benchmark in this field is NOT well developed. If a project as proposed by me is initiated, it will become a pioneer in the field. The similar idea has been adopted by University of Illinois Urbana Champaign (UIUC) and eventually has been very popular and heavily cited site. I have NOT applied for any outside funding and I do NOT have any co-researchers on the project.

During job searching, it is important to manage at least 3 letters of recommendation. Below I am copying one such issued for me:

WAYNE STATE UNIVERSITY

Department of Computer Science
College of Science
5143 Cass Avenue, Room 460 State Hall
Detroit, Michigan 48202
Voice 313-577-6783/Fax 313-577-6868

February 26, 2009
Professor Akshai Aggarwal
Director
School of Computer Science
University of Windsor
401 Sunset Avenue
Windsor, Ontario N9B 3P4

Dear Professor Aggarwal:

It is my pleasure to introduce Mr. Emdad Ahmed and write a letter of reference on his behalf. I have known Emdad since Winter of 2006 and currently serve as his major professor and dissertation director.

Emdad's research focuses on issues related to information retrieval and information integration. In particular, he is focusing on categorizing and classifying data collections into meaningful groups. This direction of research is essential in the field of autonomous information integration and data aggregation where autonomous systems collect information from internet resources having no proper labels. In such situations, query systems fail to identify required information and cause the production of wrong responses. His focus in this research is on generating useful labels for groups of data items to facilitate successful query computation.

Emdad also worked as an instructor and Graduate Teaching Assistant for several courses in our department with great success. He also once worked with me as a GTA to help me with the graduate level Database

Management course. I was pleased with his performance and the level of grasp of the subject covered. His command in English is excellent and he communicates well. His interpersonal skills and communicative ability was the key to his success as an instructor in our department. His experience in teaching undergraduate and graduate level courses will benefit in his professional career as he already has the insight and techniques one needs to posses to be a successful instructor at a department that emphasizes on both research and teaching. I have attended many of his presentations and was pleased with his style and approach. He is very articulate and quite innovative in presenting his ideas at a level an audience can receive. He has taught many Computer Science courses here at Wayne State and I am confident that he will be able to teach a wide variety of courses. In particular, I believe that he will be able to teach introductory courses in programming languages, data structures, databases, and computer networks.

Emdad has a great personality, he is aware of his strengths and weaknesses, and he is flexible and highly adaptive. He works well in a team and independently. Based on my experience, I strongly believe that Emdad will be a great addition of talent and capability in your department and prove to be an asset soon. I strongly recommend a position for him in your department.

Should there be a need for further information, please do not hesitate to contact me. I can be reached by e-mail at *jamil@cs.wayne.edu*, by phone at 313-577-6783 or by fax at 313-577-6868.

Sincerely,
Hasan Jamil, PhD
Associate Professor

In course of applying for faculty position, PhD students need to prepare *personal statement, teaching statement, research statement* etc. Below I am copying my versions in the hope that might help others in the future.

Personal Statement

Emdad Ahmed, Ph.D.
Email: *emdadahmed@hotmail.com*
Web: http://paris.cs.wayne.edu/~ay2703

Emdad Ahmed received his Ph.D. degree in Computer Science from Wayne State University (USA) in May 2011. He obtained Australian Government scholarship (AusAID) to pursue Master of Engineering Science

(MEngSc) from University of New South Wales, Australia in 1999-2001. He has received Master of Business Administration (MBA) from Institute of Business Administration, Dhaka University in 1998 and B.Sc. Engg (Computer Science and Engineering) from Bangladesh University of Engineering and Technology (BUET) in 1994 respectively. While his general research interest is in the field of Databases, Bioinformatics, his current focus is in the areas of Web data Integration. His research has resulted in several referred international conference papers, including articles that appeared in ACM WIDM, SEDE and IEEE ICSC international conferences.

As a Ph.D. student in Wayne State University, Emdad Ahmed was a recipient of several competitive awards that include Graduate Teaching Assistant, Part Time Faculty during Spring/Summer, Graduate Teaching Assistant Professional Travel award etc. He has been lecturer, Department of Computer Science and Engineering, Khulna University during 1994. He has worked as Computer Programmer (Local Consultant) in a World Bank Project, Female Secondary School Assistant Project under Directorate of Secondary and Higher Education of Ministry of Education, Bangladesh from 1994 to 1997. He has served as lecturer, Department of Electrical Engineering and Computer Science, North South University from 2001 to 2005. He has started faculty job at Montana State University Billings from Fall 2010. Currently he is an Assistant Professor of Computer Science at Cheyney University of Pennsylvania.

Emdad Ahmed is interested in doing research on cutting edge Web technologies. Specifically his PhD dissertation is on *Big Data* and *probabilistic analysis* of labeling anonymous datasets for Web data integration. There has been a paradigm shift in Web applications from static Web pages to dynamic Web applications mainly on Web form based system. Web Services are another level of abstraction where the Cloud computing infrastructure can be utilized. All these work together in concert as Software as a Service (SaaS). Emdad Ahmed has a wide spectrum of computing knowledge comprises of all the hardware and software aspects of computing. He has published a book and more than 20 research papers on Web technologies, Software Engineering, high performance computer networking, 3D graphics etc., to name a few. Given his huge exposure to the core computing field, he is willing to find tenure track position where he can make basic contribution to the knowledge of the field.

TEACHING STATEMENT

Emdad Ahmed, Ph.D.
Email: emdadahmed@hotmail.com
Web: http://paris.cs.wayne.edu/~ay2703

I graduated in Computer Science and Engineering from Bangladesh University of Engineering and Technology (BUET) obtaining first class with honors 78.2% marks. Soon after my graduation from BUET, I was appointed as Lecturer in the Computer Science and Engineering discipline of Khulna University, Bangladesh. There I conducted classes on Operating System, Numerical Analysis and Computer Simulation. I completed theoretical courses of M.Sc. Engg (computer) from BUET. Later on, to develop some managerial skill, I completed Masters of Business Administration (MBA) from Institute of Business Administration (IBA), Dhaka University, Bangladesh. Then I joined in International Islamic University, Chittagong, Bangladesh as a faculty. There I conducted courses on Database Systems and Computer Simulation/Modeling for a semester.

Australian Government advertised for a program of Masters in Computer Science and Engineering, I avail myself of this great opportunity. I was the only person selected from Bangladesh to represent my country. The masters program was a re-engineering course comprising all the aspects of hardware, software and applications. I also acted there as *tutor* for three courses in University of New South Wales: Database Systems (Oracle PL/SQL), Design and Analysis of Algorithms (implemented in Java) and Computer Networks and Applications. I was also a *teaching consult* for Design and Analysis of Algorithms course. After finishing the masters program from Australia I came back Bangladesh. Then I joined North South University as lecturer. North South University is the first private university in Bangladesh. It follows the teaching method/curriculum in close cooperation with North American standard. There I conducted several undergraduate courses:

- CSE135 Fundamentals of Computer Programming (Java)
- CSE225 Data Structures (Java and C++)
- CSC273 Theory of Computation
- CSC311/ETE335 Database Systems
- CSE325/CSE425 Programming Language Principles
- CSE326 Compiler Construction
- CSE338/ETE331 Computer Networks
- CSC348 Artificial Intelligence
- CSC373 Design and Analysis of Algorithms
- CSC382/CSE482/ETE334 Internet and Web Technology

- CSC497 Advanced Computer Networks
- CSC498/ETE498 (where I have supervised a number of undergraduate internship)
- CSC499/ETE499 (where I have supervised a number of undergraduate thesis/projects)

I started Ph.D. Program in Computer Science at Wayne State University, Detroit, USA on January 2006. There I worked as Graduate Teaching Assistant (GTA) and Instructor. I graduated in May, 2011. I have conducted classes in the Department of Computer Science, Wayne State University on the following subjects:

- CSC1050 Introduction to UNIX & C (*Lab Instructor*)
- CSC1100 Problem Solving and Programming (using Python)
- CSC1101 Problem Solving and Programming Lab (using Python) (*Lab Instructor*)
- CSC1500 Fundamental Structures of Computer Science (*Instructor*)
- CSC2000 C++ Programming (*Instructor*)
- CSC5050/ECE4050 Data Structures and Algorithms (*Instructor*)
- CSC6580 Design and Analysis of Algorithms (*Grader*)
- CSC6710 Database Management System I (*Grader*)

Besides, I used to hold office hour in Computer Science Tutoring Center. Undergraduate students are the most beneficiary of such an arrangement. I used to come to know about almost all the programming and homework assignment for a wide variety of CS courses. This has been a unique opportunity and exposure for me to stay current the recent development in CS courses and curriculum.

I took summer 2007 off from Wayne State University, that time I taught a graduate level course MCSE 6009 Internet Engineering at University of Asia Pacific, Dhaka, Bangladesh. There I also supervised two masters' students.

In Montana State University Billings, I have taught the following courses during Fall2010: CST110 Visual Basic I; CSCI109 Visual Basic I Lab; CST120 Advanced Visual Basic; CSCI111 Intermediate Java I and CMP236 Advanced Web Programming. All the above courses required hands on practical session. I enjoyed teaching and learning with the students a lot.

After completing PhD, I rejoined North South University as Assistant Professor. There I conducted the following courses: Algorithms and Data Structures; Database Systems; Internet and Web Technology; Compiler Construction and Programming Language Principles.

In Fall2012, I joined Cheyney University of Pennsylvania as Assistant Professor of Computer Science. Here I am taking classes on: Basic Principles of Computers, Computer Programming I, II, Information Structures and Intermediate Algebra. I had chance to use educational management tool like Blackboard, Desire to Learn (D2L), Power Campus, TracDat etc.

I have a particular interest in all areas of Computer Science courses. Throughout my interaction with different university's undergraduate teaching, I was able to exercise the teaching methodologies and interests. I helped create the course and the Lab for CSE326, CSC382 and CSE338 at North South University. My enthusiasm for introducing computer science problems and techniques to novice students, particularly those who may not be attracted to the field through traditional routes, means that I would enjoy teaching introductory courses, whether as a computer science survey or a programming class, or intermediate classes in data structures and algorithms. Of course, I am equipped and enthusiastic about teaching any of the computer science core courses. My research background strongly equips me for teaching upper level courses in Algorithms, Databases, Computer Networks etc. My goal in any courses I undertook would be to put into practice the teaching methodologies, while ensuring a strong integration with the department's computer science curriculum as a whole.

I enjoy teaching computer science courses tremendously and I am committed to striving for excellence in all my teaching endeavors. My teaching experience can be traced back to 1994 when I joined Khulna University as a Lecturer. My teaching skills were further polished during my two years of tutoring service in the School of Computer Science and Engineering, University of New South Wales, Australia.

From Fall2001 to Fall2005, I served as Lecturer, Department of CSE, North South University. As a teacher, we must have a clear understanding of the topics we are teaching; we must have a clear idea on how to deliver the topics to the students. Only when you know the topic well, will you be able to explain it to students well. While I was teaching, besides preparing for the class carefully, I also tried to be well organized in class, both in verbal communication and in blackboard writing as well as in power point presentation, this would certainly help the students to understand the material. As both a student and a teacher, I clearly understood that the teacher should be accessible to all students.

Besides holding regular office hours, I also allowed students to make individual appointments, email conversation. This ensured that they could seek for help whenever they needed it. Frequently, I received appreciative comments from my students about my teaching as well as my accessibility. I also think a good teacher should always look for ways to improve teaching skills. While teaching itself was certainly improving my skills, I paid great attention any suggestions either given by students or obtained from Student's Evaluation of Teaching (SET). My evaluations from students and peers have been excellent.

Looking forward, I would be interested in teaching any undergraduate computer science courses, from introductory courses in programming C/ C++/C#/ Java/ Python/ Visual Basic, Data Structures up though advanced undergraduate courses in Algorithms, Databases, Computer Networks, Internet and Web Technology to name a few. I would also enjoy teaching graduate courses in Design and Analysis of Algorithms, Web Database Integration, Advanced Computer Networks, Advanced Web Technology etc. Given my extensive experiences of using Java, PHP/MySQL, Oracle .NET etc. I will be eager to integrate these computer learning components into the teaching whenever possible, as these tools have become indispensable for both academic research and industrial applications.

RESEARCH STATEMENT

Emdad Ahmed, Ph.D.
Email: emdadahmed@hotmail.com
Web: *http://paris.cs.wayne.edu/~ay2703*

Summary of PhD Dissertation

A large number of wrappers generate tables without column names for human consumption because the meaning of the columns are apparent from the context and easy for humans to understand, but in emerging applications, labels are needed for autonomous assignment and schema mapping where machine tries to understand the tables. Autonomous label assignment is critical in volume data processing where ad hoc mediation, extraction and querying is involved.

We propose an algorithm LADS for Labeling Anonymous Datasets, which can holistically label/annotate tabular Web document. The algorithm has been tested on anonymous datasets from a number of sites, yielding very promising results. We report here our experimental results on anonymous datasets from a number of sites e.g., music, movie, watch, political, automobile, synthetic obtained through different search engine such as Google, Yahoo and MSN. The comparative probabilities of attributes being candidate labels are presented which seem to be very promising, achieved as high as 98% probability of assigning good label to anonymous attribute. To the best of our knowledge, this is the first of its kind for label assignment based on multiple search engines' recommendation. We have introduced a new paradigm, Web search engine based annotator which can holistically label tabular Web document. We categorize column into three types: disjoint set column (DSC), repeated prefix/suffix column (RPS) and numeric column (NUM). For labeling DSC column, our method relies on hit counts from Web search engine (e.g., Google, Yahoo and MSN). We formulate *speculative queries* to Web search engine and use the *principle of disambiguation by maximal evidence* to come up with our solution. Our algorithm Lads is guaranteed to work for the disjoint set column.

Experimental results from large number of sites in different domains and subjective evaluation of our approach show that the proposed algorithm LADS works fairly well. In this line we claim that our algorithm Lads is robust. In order to assign label for the Disjoint Set Column, we need a candidate set of labels (e.g., *label library*) which can be collected on-the-fly from user SQL query variable as well as from Web Form label tag. We classify a set of homogeneous anonymous datasets into meaningful label and at the same time cluster those labels into a *label library* by learning user expectation and materialization of her expectation from a site. Previous work in this field rely on *extraction ontologies*, we eliminate the need for domain specific ontologies as we could extract label from the Web form. Our system is novel in the sense that we accommodate label from the user query variable. We hypothesize that our proposed algorithm LADS will do a good job for autonomous label assignment. We bridge the gap between two orthogonal research directions: wrapper generation and ontology generation from Web site (i.e., label extraction). We are NOT aware of any such prior work that address to connect these two orthogonal research for value added services such as online comparison shopping.

Summary of major publications

So far I have published more than 20 research papers on Web Data Integration, 3D Computer Graphics, Internet and Web Technology, High Performance Computer Networking, Wireless Communication, Software Engineering and Data Engineering, Bioinformatics etc.

Web Data Integration

I have published papers in IEEE ICSC 2010 @ Carnegie Mellon University and ACM WIDM 2009 co-located with CIKM 2009 @ Hong Kong. We proposed algorithms which can holistically label tabular Web data.

Software Engineering and Data Engineering

In 2008 I had published paper on use of ontologies in Software Engineering and Data Engineering (SEDE 2008). Ontology is a popular concept in AI. According to Gruber (1993) *ontology is defined to be a formal specification of a shared conceptualization in a domain of interest.* In our thesis work, ontology is central to the query processing and reconciliation of heterogeneous online information sources. In the paper we discussed the similarity and differences in ontology vs. conceptual modeling. We argued that the entire software engineering life cycle can be augmented with ontological framework. A very good example of use of ontologies in SE is a web.xml file in J2EE environment.

Bioinformatics

I have also worked with Biologist to develop Java tool for Bioinformatics Web Data Integration and published paper in 2008 on Gene Regulatory Networks. We employed horizontal and vertical integration of Web data.

3D Computer Graphics

We published a number of papers on 3D graphics Engine. One in 2003 on scene graph management for OpenGL based 3D graphics engine. We used technique like Binary Space Partitioning (BSP tree). A start up company has been formed by one of the collaborator and patented a 3D graphics Engine called Agni3D. In 2004, we extended the research by proposing how to design an extended 3D graphics engine with features like renderer and shader. In 2005, we further extended the work on how to use programmable 3D graphics engine, how can we increase the performance of 3D games using pre calculation (we defined data structures that are changing as well as some data structures that will not change during the game environment, we can speed up the execution by pre calculated data structure)

Internet and Web Technology

In 2004, we published paper on Data Intensive Web Application (DIWA). We surveyed tools and techniques for DIWA. There are three types of latency involved in Web application: browser latency, network latency and server latency. We compared and showed performance of different database (e.g., MySQL, Oracle and SQL Server) under different circumstances.

High Performance Computer Networking

In 2005, we published a paper on performance analysis of parallel downloading from mirrored Internet sites. Parallel downloading is possible due to the nature of FTP REST command as well as thread model of HTTP range request. We studied previously proposed method in this regard and proposed a new algorithm called Dynamic Slow Start (DSS) (the name we chose from slow start algorithm in normal TCP/IP networking) for parallel downloading from mirrored Internet Sites. The proposed algorithm outperform the existing methods i.e., static equal, static unequal and dynamic method. Our proposed algorithm can be used to boost download performance in commercial download accelerator like speedbits etc.

Wireless Communication

The same work of parallel downloading has been extended in our further work in wireless networking. We studied the feasibility of the approach both in Basic Service Set (BSS) and Extended Service Set (ESS) mode of operation. We published paper in 2007 and 2008, where we have proposed to use parallel loading of Access Point (PLAP) and Mirrored Server (APMS). In 2012, we published a paper on multiple parameter based clustering in Wireless Sensor Network (WSN) using K-Means algorithm.

Summary of B.Sc Engg. Thesis

My research interest can be traced back to 1993, when I did my undergraduate thesis on Performance Analysis of Random Access Protocols by Simulation.

Carrier Sense Multiple Access with Collision Detection (CSMA/CD) and ALOHA are very well known random access communication protocol in Local Computer Networks. In this thesis work, simulation packages for the performance analysis of:

- Single Bus CSMA/CD
- Multiple Bus CSMA/CD with tree resolution
- Single Channel Pure ALOHA and Slotted ALOHA
- Multiple Channel Slotted ALOHA.

protocols have been developed. The performance parameters considered are delay, throughput and utilization. Independent parameters are chosen to be number of buses, number of stations and packet generation rate (*we used negative exponential distribution*). Varying the performance parameters with different values of these independent variables are compared. From this comparison an optimum set of parameters can be obtained for a LAN system with given configurations. The performance of all these protocols have been obtained from the simulators, programmed for different protocols, using the C programming Language. Results of the simulators have been validated using the *fairness test* and the comparison with the *analytical result*. The developed simulators can be used to predict the delay, throughput and utilization of the above mentioned protocols networks of any length, with any number of stations and for any transmission speed. *The most interesting outcome of the thesis was that using our proposed algorithm/ scheme i.e., CSMA/CD with tree resolution, the normalized delay was shown to be half than that of slotted ALOHA, of course by sacrificing a little bit of utilization of the network. In our case, we were able to achieve a maximum utilization of 33%, whereas in slotted ALOHA it is about 36% (1/e).*

Research, Articles, Book and Publications

1. **Emdad Ahmed,** "Labeling Anonymous Datasets", ISBN 978-3-659-26056-8 Published by Lap Lambert Academic Publishing, Germany, October 11, 2012
2. Asif Khan, Tamim Iqbal, **Emdad Ahmed,** Muhammad Abdul Awal, "Mulitple Parameter based Clustering (MPC): Prospective Analysis for Wireless Sensor Network (WSN) using K-Means Algorithm", International Journal of Wireless Sensor Network, pp 18-24, Vol 4, No 1, January 2012
3. **Emdad Ahmed**, "Teaching and Learning Computer Science for the last 23 years", in ACM ICPC Dhaka Site Magazine, Department of Electrical Engineering and Computer Science (EECS), North South University (NSU), Dhaka, Bangladesh, pp 1-3, November 18-19, 2011
4. **Emdad Ahmed,** "Achieving Classification and Clustering in One Shot-Lesson Learned from Labeling Anonymous Datasets", paper published in the 5th Computer Science Conference (CSC 2011), University of Windsor, Ontario, CANADA, April 21, 2011, pp 1-4
5. **Emdad Ahmed**, "Post Processing Wrapper Generated Tables for Labeling Anonymous Datasets", PhD Dissertation, pp 1-92, Department of Computer Science, Wayne State University, USA, December, 2010
6. **Emdad Ahmed,** "Achieving Classification and Clustering in One Shot-Lesson Learned from Labeling Anonymous Datasets", paper published in the 4th IEEE International Conference of Semantic

Computing (ICSC 2010), Carnegie Mellon University, USA, September 22-24, 2010, pp 228-231

7. Shammi Akhtar, **Emdad Ahmed,** Aloke Kumar Saha, Kazi Shamsul Arefin, "Performance Analysis of Integrated Service over Differentiated Service for Next Generation Internet", in Journal of Computer and Information Technology (JCIT), ISSN 2078-5828, pp 95-101, July 2010.
8. **Emdad Ahmed**, Hasan M. Jamil, "Post Processing Wrapper Generated Tables for Labeling Anonymous Datasets", PhD Dissertation pre-Defense Technical Report, pp 1-145, Department of Computer Science, Wayne State University, USA, July 14, 2010
9. Kazi Shamsul Arefin, **Emdad Ahmed**, M. Fayyaz Khan, Mahbub Ahmed, Aloke Kumar Saha, "Performance Analysis of Parallel Download on Job Scheduling in Time Sharing Environment", paper published in the 2nd International Conference on Engineering Education for Sustainable Development (ICEESD 2009), Dhaka, Bangladesh, December 19-20, 2009, pp 1-6
10. **Emdad Ahmed**, Hasan M. Jamil, "Post Processing Wrapper Generated Tables for Labeling Anonymous Datasets", in 11th International Workshop on Web Information and Data Management, (WIDM'09), co-located with ACM CIKM 2009, Hong Kong, November 2-6, 2009, pp 63-66.
11. **Emdad Ahmed**, Hasan M. Jamil, "Resource Capability Discovery/ Description Management System—Labeling Anonymous Dataset for Web Data Integration", PhD Prospectus Exam Technical Report, pp 1-54, Department of Computer Science, Wayne State University, USA, February 16, 2009
12. **Emdad Ahmed,** "Resource Capability Discovery and Description Management System for Bioinformatics Data and Service Integration—An Experiment with Gene Regulatory Networks", paper accepted for publication in the 11th International Conference on Computer and Information Technology (ICCIT), pp 70-75, Technical co-sponsor IEEE Bangladesh Section, Khulna, December 25-27, 2008
13. **Emdad Ahmed**, "Bioinformatics Web Data and Service Integration—An Experiment with Gene Regulatory Networks", paper accepted for publication in the 5th International Conference on Electrical and Computer Engineering (ICECE 2008) Technical co-sponsor IEEE Bangladesh Section, Dhaka, December 20-22, 2008 pp 56-61
14. **Emdad Ahmed**, "Use of Ontologies in Software Engineering", paper published in the 17th International Conference on Software

Engineering and Data Engineering, SEDE 2008, LA, ISCA, USA, June 30-July 2, 2008, pp 145-150.

15. Kazi Shamsul Arefin, **Emdad Ahmed**, *Md.* Zahangir Alom **"Cross-Layer Design of Wireless Networking for Parallel Loading of Access Points and Mirrored Servers (APMS)"** paper published in the International Conference on Electronics, Computer and Communication (ICECC), Rajshahi, Bangladesh, June 27-29, 2008
16. Kazi Shamsul Arefin, **Emdad Ahmed**, "Cross-Layer Design of Wireless Networking for Parallel Loading of Access Points (PLAP)" paper published in the 10th International Conference on Computer and Information Technology (ICCIT 2007), Technical Co-sponsor IEEE, Bangladesh section, Dhaka, Bangladesh, December 27-29, 2007
17. **Emdad Ahmed**, Hasan M. Jamil, "A Survey on Bioinformatics Data and Service Integration Using Ontology and Declarative Workflow Query Language", PhD Qualifying Exam Technical Report, pp 1-67, Department of Computer Science, Wayne State University, USA, March 2007
18. Md. Tawhid Bin Waez, Sadrul Habib Chowdhury, **Emdad Ahmed**, Miftahur Rahman, "Performance Analysis of Parallel Downloading from Mirrored Internet Sites" paper published in the Proceedings of the 8th International Conference on Computer and Information Technology (ICCIT) Dhaka, Dec 28-30, 2005 pp 222-227 (*2nd best Paper Award*)
19. M Mahmud Hasan, M Sazzad Karim, **Emdad Ahmed** "Generating and Rendering Procedural Clouds in Real Time on Programmable 3D Graphics Hardware" paper published in the Proceedings of the 9th IEEE International Multi Topic Conference (INMIC) National University of Computer and Emerging Sciences, Karachi Campus, Pakistan, December 23-25, 2005
20. Abdullah Al Mazed, Mirza Hasan Asif, **Emdad Ahmed**, "INCREASING PERFORMANCE OF 3D GAMES USING PRECALCULATION" paper published in the Proceedings of the 9th IEEE International Multi Topic Conference (INMIC) National University of Computer and Emerging Sciences, Karachi Campus, Pakistan, December 23-25, 2005
21. Hasan Mahmud, Sazzad Karim, **Emdad Ahmed** "Design of an Extended 3D Graphics Engine" paper published in 3rd International Conference on Electrical and Computer Engineering (ICECE) Technical co-sponsor IEEE Bangladesh Section, pp 581-584, Dhaka, December 28-30, 2004

22. K. M. Ibrahim Asif, **Emdad Ahmed**, Dr. Miftahur Rahman "Performance Analysis of Data Intensive Web Application (DIWA)—A Case Study" Paper published in 7th International Conference on Computer and Information Technology (ICCIT), pp 226-231, Dhaka, December 26-28, 2004.
23. Adnan M. L. Karim, Sazzad Karim, **Emdad Ahmed**, M. Rokonuzzaman "Scene graph Management for OpenGL based 3D Graphics Engine" paper published in 6th International Conference on Computer and Information Technology (ICCIT), pp 395-400, vol I, Dhaka, December 19-21, 2003.
24. **Emdad Ahmed**, M. Anisuzzaman, Kamrul Islam M. Naser, Dr. Md. Shamsul Alam ``Performance Study of Random Access Protocols by Simulation" unpublished B.Sc. Engg Thesis, Department of Computer Science and Engineering, Bangladesh University of Engineering and Technology (BUET), Dhaka, December 1993.

STATEMENT ILLUSTRATING COMMITMENT TO FOSTERING CAMPUS RACIAL DIVERSITY

EMDAD AHMED, Ph.D.
Email: *emdadahmed@hotmail.com*
Web: http://paris.cs.wayne.edu/~ay2703

I had always interest for mathematics and science from very beginning of my schooling. I obtained scholarship/stipend when I was in *grade eight*. I passed my Secondary School Certificate (SSC) in 1985 first division with distinction in four subjects obtaining 75% marks. Then I got myself admitted in higher secondary education in the best college in my home city. I passed my Higher Secondary Certificate (HSC) exam in 1987 obtaining 82.4% marks and stood 15th among some 100000 students. I made up my mind to be a computing professional.

During 1988, I heard Bangladesh University of Engineering and Technology (BUET), the only technological university in Bangladesh, is going to introduce Bachelor in Computer Science and Engineering (CSE) program for the first time in our home country, Bangladesh. After a thorough admission procedure, only top most 4000 students were allowed to sit for admission test and among them only top most 30 students were admitted in CSE, BUET. It was my rare fortune that *I stood first* among those students.

I was interested in computer networks and application, RDBMS, computer simulation etc. To fulfill my passion, I took thesis titled *Performance Study of Random Access protocols by Simulation*. There I extensively studied and developed simulator to predict behavior of LAN

Ethernet protocol CSMA/CD and AHOLA protocol. **I graduated in Computer Science and Engineering** from BUET obtaining *first class with honors 78.2% marks and 7th position.*

Soon after my graduation from BUET, I was appointed as Lecturer, Computer Science and Engineering discipline, Khulna University. There I conducted classes on operating system, numerical analysis and computer simulation. In the meantime, World Bank (international bank for reconstruction and development) initiated a nationwide project, Female Secondary School Assistance Project (FSSAP) under the ministry of education, Bangladesh. I was appointed as Local Consultant (computer programmer). There I in a team of international/local consultant, data processing manage, computer programmers, system analyst developed Educational Management Information System (EMIS). Here I gained practical experience in RDBMS.

In the meantime, **I completed theoretical courses of M.Sc. Engg (computer) from BUET.** Later to develop some managerial skill, **I completed Masters of Business Administration (MBA)** majoring in development management from Institute of Business Administration (IBA), Dhaka University. My contract with the project was over. Then I joined in International Islamic University, Chittagong. There I conducted courses on database systems and computer simulation/modeling for a semester.

Australian Government advertised for a program to do **Masters in computer science and engineering,** I avail myself of this great opportunity. I was the only person selected from Bangladesh to represent my country. The masters program was a re-engineering course comprising all the aspects of hardware, software and applications. I also acted there as *tutor* for three courses in University of New South Wales; database systems (oracle PL/SQL), design and analysis of algorithms (implemented in JAVA) and Computer Networks and applications. I was also a *teaching consult* for design and analysis of algorithms course.

After finishing the masters program from Australia, as promised I came back Bangladesh. Then I joined North South University as lecturer. North South University is the *first private university* in Bangladesh. It follows the teaching method/curriculum in close cooperation with North American standard. Here I have conducted 12 courses viz. CSE135; CSE225; CSC273; CSC311; CSC325; CSE326; CSE338; CSC348; CSC373; CSC382, CSC497; CSC499. I have supervised a number of undergraduate thesis/ projects. I have published a number of papers in International Conference on Computer and Information Technology (ICCIT 2003, 2004, 2005, 2007, 2008) and also in International Conference on Electrical and Computer Engineering (ICECE 2004, 2008). I have published research papers in the IEEE INMIC 2005, SEDE 2008, ACM WIDM 2009, IEEE ICSC 2010 etc.

I have done some advanced courses like Network Routing and Switching, Advanced Computer Networks; Computer Graphics using a GUI toolkit etc. I have a very strong background in network simulation, Distributed Database Management Systems, Web Data Integration and Bioinformatics. I intend to continue research on any one of those.

For the last five years (2006-2010), while pursuing PhD in Computer Science, I have been Graduate Teaching Assistant (GTA) at Wayne State University (WSU), Detroit, Michigan. WSU is situated in metropolitan Detroit, it provides world class education. I had been very fortunate to interact with academic diversity from an array of student populations: American, Asian, Middle Eastern etc.

Platteville is the largest city in *Grant County* in southwestern *Wisconsin*. The city is home to the *University of Wisconsin-Platteville*. The racial makeup of the city is 96.15% *White*, 1.12% *Black* or *African American*, 0.27% *Native American*, 1.40% *Asian*, 0.04% *Pacific Islander*, 0.27% from *other races*, and 0.75% from two or more races. 0.88% of the populations were *Hispanic* or *Latino* of any race. Platteville is mainly a college town, with some development in the white-collar sector. That growth is a result of the increasing number of engineering firms locating in Platteville to take advantage of UW-P's engineering program. *University of Wisconsin-Platteville* is committed to creating a culture of campus racial **diversity** that can enable faculty and students to respond to the complexities of the contemporary United States and the larger international community. Cultivating a culture of campus racial **diversity** means more than improving statistical representation of demographic minorities. Yet it is clear that demographic, campus racial **diversity** has an impact on the development of the curriculum and the richness of critical inquiry on campus. Studies have confirmed that engaging people from a broad mixture of social, **racial**, and religious backgrounds improves learning outcomes among students. A diverse faculty and student body stimulates new perspectives and questions within the liberal arts tradition. Living and learning in a diverse community challenges conventional ways of thinking and response. Such experience will prepare *University of Wisconsin-Platteville* graduates to act as leaders in all sectors of society and enhances their ability to contribute to the common good as informed citizens. Faculty can learn new approaches to their subjects from other faculty and students, and thus expand their horizons of research and inquiry. A culture of campus racial **diversity** thus will foster an innovative curriculum that fulfills the *University of Wisconsin-Platteville*'s core mission.

Throughout my educational career, I have been very fortunate to interact with a huge cultural, ethnic and racial diversity. I am firmly committed to fostering *University of Wisconsin-Platteville*'s campus racial diversity.

I thought I would write about 150 pages for the book. The first 100 pages I could write very quickly. Then remaining 50 pages started to give me hard time. Then I started to mix with diversified group of people other than my area of expertise. Mixing with different background people sometimes click ideas. Everything is in my memory/brain the only thing lacking is that of click in the nick of time. Am I wasting my time? Who will ever read it? I remember when I submitted my PhD dissertation, I said my advisor that who is going to read my dissertation (I was pointing the question to the committee members). My advisor confidently said that all the committee members will read it thoroughly before signing it. And the statement is true: there was a form from graduate school which says to sign the committee members and by signing they are confirming that they have read the dissertation and it is ready to final defense. So I hope my endeavor to write a book will be successful sometime. Actually I wanted to make the book a complete package and life story of a graduate student.

Turing Award is named after famous computer scientist Allan Turing. The award in computer science is considered similar to noble prize in general academic discipline. In the year 2011, Turing Award was given to *Judea Pearl* for his basic contribution of probabilistic reasoning/analysis in AI. I remember in Artificial Intelligence I used the concept of *information gain* (i.e., entropy) during pruning search space tree. The essence of this is just to use Bayesian theorem to infer unknown probability from known facts. My PhD dissertation happened to use the same principle.

I have to stop writing otherwise as time goes by I wish to add more and more stories of my daily life. I sincerely hope that the time I spent writing the book will benefit the next generation of Computer Science graduate. In the book I heavily used a lot of terms which I deliberately italicized to emphasize the importance. I strongly believe a Computer Science student should have rigorous amount of academic training to be successful in practical life. I will welcome any of the readers of the book to contact me at *emdadahmed@hotmail.com.* This is a promise from me just refer to the email heading "The Art of Getting Computer Science PhD", your reply is guaranteed for life.

www.ingramcontent.com/pod-product-compliance
Lightning Source LLC
Chambersburg PA
CBHW051252050326
40689CB00007B/1165
* 9 7 8 1 4 7 9 7 8 9 6 4 1 *